PENGUI

ALAN BROWNJOHN was
elementary and grammar s
has given readings of his
works as a senior lecturer
tion. His books of poems are *The Railings* (1961), *The Lions' Mouths* (1967), and *Sandgrains on a Tray* (1969).

MICHAEL HAMBURGER was born in 1924 in Berlin. In 1933 he moved to Edinburgh, then to London, becoming a British subject in 1939. He went to Westminster School and Christ Church, Oxford, and, after army service, worked as a free-lance writer and odd-job man from 1948 to 1952. Until 1964 he was lecturer in German at the universities of London and Reading. Since then he has been living as a writer, with only temporary teaching appointments; in 1966–7 he was Purington Lecturer at Mount Holyoke College, Massachusetts. He has twice been awarded Bollingen Foundation fellowships, and has won three prizes for his work as a translator. Since his first book appeared in 1943 his books of poems have included *Flowering Cactus* (1950), *The Dual Site* (1958), *Weather and Season* (1963), and *Travelling* (1969). His critical books include *Reason and Energy* (1957), *From Prophecy to Exorcism* (1966), and *The Truth of Poetry* (1969), and his translations, mainly of poems, include versions of Hölderlin, Baudelaire, and twentieth century German poets. Michael Hamburger is married and has three children.

CHARLES TOMLINSON was born in 1927 in Stoke-on-Trent and educated at Queen's College, Cambridge. He is now reader in English poetry at the University of Bristol. His books are *Relations and Contraries* (1951), *The Necklace* (1955), *Seeing Is Believing* (1960); *Versions from Tyutchev* (1960), *Castilian Ilexes: Versions from Machado* (1963) – both with Henry Gifford; *A Peopled Landscape* (1963), and *American Scenes* (1966). Teacher, critic, and a painter, Charles Tomlinson has lived in London, Italy, America, Somerset and Gloucestershire. He is married and has two daughters.

Penguin Modern Poets

14

ALAN BROWNJOHN
MICHAEL HAMBURGER
CHARLES TOMLINSON

Penguin Books

Penguin Books Ltd, Harmondsworth, Middlesex, England
Penguin Books Inc., 7110 Ambassador Road, Baltimore, Maryland 21207, U.S.A.
Penguin Books Australia Ltd, Ringwood Victoria, Australia

—

This selection first published 1969
Reprinted 1970

—

—

Made and printed in Great Britain by
C. Nicholls & Company Ltd
Set in Monotype Garamond

Contents

CONTENTS

ACKNOWLEDGEMENTS

The poems in this selection are taken from the following books, to whose publishers acknowledgement is made: *The Lions' Mouths* (1967), by Alan Brownjohn, published by Macmillan & Co. Ltd and in America by Dufour Editions Inc.; *The Railings* (1961), by Alan Brownjohn, published by The Digby Press; *Flowering Cactus* and *Poems* 1950–51, by Michael Hamburger, published by The Hand and Flower Press, Aldington, Kent; *The Dual Site* (1958), by Michael Hamburger, published by Routledge & Kegan Paul Ltd; *Weather and Season* (1958), by Michael Hamburger, published by Longmans, Green & Co. Ltd and in America by Atheneum Publishers; *The Necklace* (1966), *A Peopled Landscape* (1963), *American Scenes* (1966), by Charles Tomlinson, published by Oxford University Press; *Seeing is Believing* (1960), by Charles Tomlinson, published by Oxford University Press and in America reprinted by arrangement with Astor-Honor, Inc., New York.

ALAN BROWNJOHN

ALAN BROWNJOHN

The Railings

Once there would have been the woman standing
Between the trees behind the dancing railings as he walked,
But that is not now so.

And once there would have been
A hope of the woman, a figment of the branches
As they shifted with the light –
That might have been, that might have been,
But neither is this any longer true.

Not even now is the hope what it was,
And will not regain the face:
Two years, three years, the walk could go
While only the principle of the woman

Faintly remained. And that would scarcely be enough.

The principle will drain from out a place.
The hope will have to go to other things.

Two Poems after Prévert

I

In this city, perhaps a street.
In this street, perhaps a house.
In this house, perhaps a room
And in this room a woman sitting,
Sitting in the darkness, sitting and crying
For someone who has just gone through the door
And who has just switched off the light
Forgetting she was there.

II

We are going to see the rabbit.
We are going to see the rabbit,
Which rabbit, people say?
Which rabbit, ask the children?
Which rabbit?
The only rabbit,
The only rabbit in England,
Sitting behind a barbed-wire fence
Under the floodlights, neon lights,
Sodium lights,
Nibbling grass
On the only patch of grass
In England, in England
(Except the grass by the hoardings
Which doesn't count.)
We are going to see the rabbit
And we must be there on time.

First we shall go by escalator,
Then we shall go by underground,
And then we shall go by motorway
And then by helicopterway,
And the last ten yards we shall have to go
On foot.

And now we are going
All the way to see the rabbit,
We are nearly there,
We are longing to see it,
And so is the crowd
Which is here in thousands
With mounted policemen
And big loudspeakers
And bands and banners,
And everyone has come a long way.
But soon we shall see it
Sitting and nibbling
The blades of grass
On the only patch of grass
In – but something has gone wrong!
Why is everyone so angry,
Why is everyone jostling
And slanging and complaining?

The rabbit has gone,
Yes, the rabbit has gone.
He has actually burrowed down into the earth
And made himself a warren, under the earth,
Despite all these people.
And what shall we do?
What *can* we do?

It is all a pity, you must be disappointed,
Go home and do something else for today,
Go home again, go home for today.
For you cannot hear the rabbit, under the earth,
Remarking rather sadly to himself, by himself,
As he rests in his warren, under the earth:
'It won't be long, they are bound to come,
They are bound to come and find me, even here.'

Retirement

The middle-afternoon is the worst of the blanks.
Shuffle the four equal armies of the contentious cards
And manoeuvre those. Or failing that, indict for yourself
In a never-to-be-written recollection, your successful
Colleague of some brisk campaign. The minor consolations
Of the manageable evening arrive the faster
For either, or both, of these applications of power.

Snow in Bromley

As of some unproved right, the snow
Settles the outer suburbs now,
Laying its claim unhurriedly
On gnome and monkey-puzzle-tree.

Observe its power to shape and build,
Even in this unfruitful world,
Its white informal fantasies,
From roofs and paths and rockeries.

And swayed by such soft moods, I fall
Into forgiving nearly all
The aspirations of the place,
And what it does to save its face:

The calm and dutiful obsession
With what is 'best in our position',
The loyal and realistic views,
The rush-hours with the *Evening News* –

The snow fulfils its pure design
And softens every ugly line,
And for a while will exorcize
These virulent proprieties.

Within one mile of here there is
No lovelier place to walk than this,
On days when these kind flakes decide
That what it boasts of, they shall hide.

For a Journey

House Field, Top Field, Oak Field, Third Field:
Though maps conclude their duties, the names trek on
Unseen across every county. Farmers call hillocks
And ponds and streams and lanes and rocks
By the first words to hand; a heavy, whittled-down
Simplicity meets the need, enough to help say
Where has yielded best, or the way they walked from home.

You can travel safely over land so named –
Where there is nowhere that could not somewhere
Be found in a memory which knows, and loves.
So watch then, all the more carefully, for
The point where the pattern ends: where mountains, even,
And swamps and forests and gaping bays acquire
The air of not needing ever to be spoken of.

Who knows what could become of you where
No one has understood the place with names?

William Empson at Aldermaston

This is our dead sea, once a guidebook heath.
Left and right hands worked busily together
A parliament or two,
And there she stands:

Twelve miles of cooling pipes; concrete and secret
Warrens underground; clean little towers
Clamped with strong ladders; red, brisk vans
Which hurry round

The wide, kerbed avenues with pulsing lights
To signify danger; and all this
Extending still its miles, as seas possessed
Of power or anger

Will – except that here
The tide decrees, with threats in yellow paint,
Its own unquestioned bounds, keeps dogs to catch
Someone who gets

Beyond the fence: it seems that otherwise
We shiver from an unclean nakedness,
And need to clothe our hot emotions cold
With wire, and curs.

But let there be some praise, where that is due:
For paint, of enlivening colours, spent
On all these deathly offices. Where typists sit,
Who do not make the thing,

Or scientists, who do not fire the thing,
Or workers, who obey the scientists,
The rooms are beautiful. And anyone
Who passed by car one day

Not knowing what it was would never guess.
(Perhaps some urgent public undertaking
Set up for health, or water? Or a camp
Where other people went

On holidays?) Such airs of carnival,
With death designed as smiling, to conceal
His proper features – these things justified
Replies in kind:

An absurd fête of life, in one Friday field
For which no pass was needed. The effect:
Two sorts of carnival clashing: on this side
The mud, or grass,

The boots and stoves and caravans; that side,
The trim, discreet pavilions of the State.
And one more contrast marked these gaieties:
This side there seemed

Some thousands, while of death's there wasn't one.
Just the white-braided police returned the stare
Of the boys with haversacks, or the fierce
Empirical gaze

Of the man with the Chinese beard, or the pondering glance
Of the woman with the basket on wheels.
And some thought death's precise executives
Had told or asked

The servants of his will to stay away,
Hinting of jobs they might not like to lose,
And they had houses . . . from whose windows, next,
Many faces looked the way

Of the procession; speaking not a word,
But merely watching. How else, then, explain
If this was not the reason, why their children,
Through all the bands and singing,

All the beards and the guitars, did not come out;
But stood behind held curtains, listlessly,
With tight and puzzled faces, or peered through
Some furtive upstairs sunblind

While it passed? No coloured hat, not one
In all the range of shirts and slogans worn,
Seemed odder than these faces. That deep blankness
Was the real thing strange.

If Time's to Work

Because there is somebody washing below,
This tap rasps in its throat. I say again,
I should not really let my hands expect
Water at any time; yet despair must show
If this unnerving guttural cough has wrecked
My strenuous answer to the morning's rain.

The week has stopped at one cold point of day
By the empty bowl; the mirror holds and keeps,
For longer than it should, its uncombed image;
The razor which I hold must shave away
More parts of night; but at this arid stage,
Night seems to have returned, all action sleeps.

And time, it seems to me, now that I wait
Leaning in one white corner, crouched and still,
Means merely, What contains activity:
Those areas of waking which create
The sense of moving, doing, constantly,
However small the purpose they fulfil.

One unexpected pause in this will cheat
Time of such meaning as it can convey:
Minutes, deprived of their brief purposes,
Pass vacantly, no sign to indicate
You lived in every one of them: there is
No kind of time which these blank wastes obey.

If time's to work, it needs the tap to run,
And with its failure had this thought arrived:
In death, too, there may be no more than this,
No certain state of being lost or won
For world or silence – just some endless pause,
And into it, no message dropped to say,

Move to the next brief act which must be lived.

Balance

The ceremonious dispositions of hands
In the hushed air of blessing, in prayer,
In particular moments of love,

Contain the exactest peace. Their calm preserves
A dedicated poise: each holy act
Quietly instinct with deep restraint and tact.

They know they must not falter and betray
What is behind their skill. Their wisdom serves
To hold them back from gestures not in tune.

And so, for a short time, they do not tumble
Down from the ceremonious to the true:
They hover still; just manage not to show

That blessing very often condescends,
And prayer pleads up from self-wrought misery,
And love's hands can reach after loveless ends.

By Daytime

(FOR K.S.T.)

That one we speak of who would harm the sense
If we lay out in her by night and slept,
Is certainly tamed now; has nothing on
The uncomplicated sun;

Has by day no power
Quite equal to the beam which there
Distinguishes the sharp lake from the trees,
And clearly colours the heather
We do not gather.

She inhabits absentmindedly a sky
Not at all her own, ill-fitted to invoke
Her customary presences, and tides;

Seems almost of not much importance any more,
Though we should be fair
To her drained face,
Should admit that it has not been

A day or a place or a mood to worry out
A just opinion of the moon.

The Situation

For it was that the cousins never came,
And so we could not know what they were like.
They never did walk out in their overwhelming way
To stand by the streaming water-butt, or
To hold the fence with their girls' adult hands.
This garden can't be remembered having them laughing,
So they remain a possibility:
That after our disappointment with man
And with dogs and with travel and with remaining still,
From our last armchairs we shall come to know
That there are the cousins left; who, that day,
Were to come, and did not, and are there to be tried yet.

Farmer's Point of View

I own certain acre-scraps of woodland, scattered
On undulating ground; enough to lie hidden in. So,

About three times a year, and usually August,
Pairs of people come to one or another patch. They stray

Around the edges first, plainly wanting some excuse
To go on in; then talking, as if not concerned,

And always of something else, not what they intend,
They find their way, by one or another approach,

To conducting sexual liaisons – on *my* land.
I've tried to be careful. I haven't mentioned 'love'

Or any idea of passion or consummation;
And I won't call them 'lovers' because I can't say

If they come from affection, or lust, or blackmail,
Or if what they do has any particular point

For either or both (and who can say what 'love' means?)
So what am I saying? I'd like to see people pondering

What unalterable acts they might be committing
When they step down, full of plans, from their trains or cars.

I am not just recording their tragic, or comic, emotions,
Or even the subtler hazards of owning land –

I am honestly concerned. I want to say, politely,
That I worry when I think what they're about:

I want them to explain themselves before they use my woods.

1939

Where the ball ran into the bushes,
And I was sent to find it, being
Useful for that more than to play their game,
I saw instead
This badge, from someone's brother, in
Some regiment of that war: a trophy
Begged for and polished, coveted certainly,
But lost now, slightly touched with dust already,
Yet shining still, under smooth leaves drab with dust.
I knew that people prized such trophies then,
It was the way of all of us. I might,
For no one looked, have taken it
For mine. I valued it. It shone
For me as much as anyone.
And yet some fear or honesty, some sense
It wasn't to be mine – it wasn't more –
Said No to all of this. Besides,
They shouted in the distance for their ball.
For once quite quickly, I
Made up my mind
And left the thing behind.

Ode to Felix

At that tired eye-level point where
Impulse buying starts, he
Was there in flush, banked rows in
The supermarket: Felix the Cat.

Two dozen cat-food packets, patterned
For sales appeal, repeated two
Dozen static gestures of his face who
Almost first made cartoons animate.

I remembered that black-and-white
Stroll, brought back on the t.v. screen
About twenty years after: undoubtedly
Smart for its time, the commentator said.

Yes, he had all the possibilities
Already, little early Felix. His
Famous walk was even then the quaint, quick
Cartoon swagger, his features were

The easy prototype of all
Those smirking descendants, capering
In slick, flourished lines, richer
For the primary colours, and running on

Down and down a million celluloid frames
Hand-painted in endless studio rows by
Patient, paid artists reducing everything to
That clear-cut, lucid world, while

Elsewhere other grown men sound-tracked
The basic squawk. – This way was
The world infested by your
Charming animal kingdom, Felix, having

Driven out real beasts. Numberless
American children responded to
The uncle-funny voices, actually came
To look like Mickey Mouse. In the

Demure eyes of innumerable
Homely girls and wives lived
Bambi's primal innocence. Felix,
You were first of all those lovably

Blundering and resourceless dogs and
Elephants who helped to make our
Gross and failing natures bearable.
You set off Li'l Abner, firm and strait,

Shouldering over fields with no effort, as in
Our own fulfilment dreams, you
Tamed with Snow White all our dwarfs
And witches, you helped to paint

Donald Duck on the fuselage of
The bomber for Hiroshima. If today
A man in the *Sunday Times* Colour
Supplement makes t.v. commercials

To pay to make his very own cartoon
Satirizing agencies, the credit's
Partly yours, and you can be proud to think your
Walt Disney voted for Goldwater . . .

I would not buy your food, I have no cat.
I can pass on down the stacked and shining
Aisles to other violences (the frozen red
Chops glossed in cellophane on puce, plastic trays)

But I'm not to pass without that sense, again,
Of one of my more elementary sorts of
Going mad: Your thousands of representatives,
Felix, walking into my world, writing my

Morning letters, modulating from the shapes
Of strangers outside the house, answering
My alarm calls for Fire, Police, *Ambulance*. In
That last nightmare trap and maze, they

Strut and chirp their obscene, unstoppable
Platitudes, Felix, while I run round and
Round and round to destroy their pert, joking smiles
And scream my own voice hoarse into their cute squeak.

Trio

He has now gone with the toy gun into the greengrocer's shop
And is using some mock ploy with the greengrocer's girl.
She is cramped up, uncomfortably half-sat on the long ledge
Of the frozen food Cool Cabinet. She looks
A suitable imitation of absolute fright, she raises
Her hands and gives a visible but inaudible shout
– The traffic is so loud – as he gestures with the Xmas gun
Towards the celery or the till. She is a tall excitable
Girl of the kind wearing tinted, attenuated glasses
And patchy coloured nails. He is thick, blunt, overcoated
Wedge of a middle-class man with several parcels,
Including the toy gun. Now suddenly the proprietor, in a green coat,
Comes out of the store at the back and throws a horrified stare,
And shrinks himself, trembling, against the potatoes
In their brown, stolid banks. The man with the wooden red gun
Speaks, you can see, but you can't hear anything he says,
And all of them are standing in these postures still,
As they might be if the gorgon glance of a photographer
Had taken them all in flagrant tableau to present to the future:
On Xmas Eve, behind the green leaves and pink paper
Of the lighted trade window of 'Mackin's Best Fruit', between
Frozen plaice fillets and South African oranges.

The Preservation

It's quite worth keeping your surprise at the untrodden
Snow on the long step that particular winter night
– As if we had been indoors for days –

As in that time your every movement told,
And looked responsible. Never had your feet
Set out their marks on things with such grave care,

Or honour of any place. And all the mocking
Extensions to words in your hands' actions
Drained right away, or were absolved

In one cupped, simple gesture, collecting
(To taste and to smile) some snow in a quick mild heap
From the near top of the street wall.

A Hairdresser's

Something I remember from six is
Waiting for mother to dry, sat with
Home Chat and knitting books to read while
The warm cage glowed round her settled hair.

That was in a corner up in a
Room above the Gentlemen's Saloon,
Out of the way. But they *exhibit*
Them now, as here, turning magazines

Under the gesturing fingers of
Their talkative priestesses. Tall glass
In the High Street, florid with pot-plants,
Sets the new style: Huge, groomed photographs

And offers of 'Life restored'. It's a
'Fine art', you couldn't relate it to
Any usefulness; in this, having
Less of a function, even, than some

Oildom's backscratcher, following his
Chevrolet to the gaming tables
In a Super Snipe. I wish to feel
My complaint is better than a mere

Chafing memory of a child's hours
Waiting and waiting; it sees the point
With a cool rationality; it has
The courage to reject some things....

But – 'If they want to', drones out some
Fool-libertarian voice, 'let them. Why
Shouldn't they do as they like?' (You
Have heard – or maybe used – that very tone!)

Passing in High Street rain, I repeat
My glance at that window and its line
Of faces locked in hives. No. I can't
Wish I were as liberal as that.

Skipping Rhyme

Pain of the leaf, one, two –
Word of the stone, three, four –
Foot of the dark, pit of the hand,
Heart of the cloud, five, six, and
Out!
    Skip.
Nora she had white eyes,
Mary she had black –
Helen looked in Grey Man's Wood and
Never came
Back!
    Jump.
Nora draws a green thread,
Mary spins it blue –
But Helen will not bind it till her
True Love makes it
True!
    Quick!
One, two, leaf of the pain,
Three, four, stone of the word,

/ / / / / /
Five, six, dark of the foot, hand of the pit,
/ / /
Cloud of the heart, and
/
OUT!

Class Incident from Graves

Wednesdays were guest night in the mess, when the colonel expected the married officers, who usually dined at home, to attend. The band played Gilbert and Sullivan music behind a curtain.... Afterwards the bandmaster was invited to the senior officer's table for his complimentary glass of Light or Vintage. (*Good-bye to All That*)

At the officers' table, for half an hour afterwards, port,
The bandmaster. He accepts, one drink long,
All the courtesy of the gentlemen. They are suave, and equal.

'I expect with your job... Do you find... Oh well....'
The bandmaster edges the shining inch of port along the grain of the table,
Precisely covering one knot with the transparent
Base of the glass. He crouches forward over the polished wood
Towards the officers, not comfortably convivial,
Eyes always going to the face speaking next,
Deferential, very pleased.
The band put away their instruments out at the back, having

Drunk their beers standing.
The detachable pieces of brass lie down
In the felt grooves of the cases, just as they should.
Nine-thirty strikes.
There is laughter of men together, coming from inside.
'Mitchell's still in there, hob-nobbing with the officers.'

Office Party

We were throwing out small-talk
On the smoke-weary air,
When the girl with the squeaker
Came passing each chair.

She was wearing a white dress,
Her paper-hat was a blue
Crown with a red tassel,
And to every man who

Glanced up at her, she leant over
And blew down the hole,
So the squeaker inflated
And began to unroll.

She stopped them all talking
With this trickery,
And she didn't leave out anyone
Until she came to me.

I looked up and she met me
With a half-teasing eye
And she took a mild breath and
Went carefully by,

And with cold concentration
To the next man she went,
And squawked out the instrument
To its fullest extent.

And whether she passed me
Thinking that it would show
Too much favour to mock me
I never did know –

Or whether her withholding
Was her cruelty,
And it was that she despised me,
I couldn't quite see –

So it could have been discretion,
And it could have been disgust,
But it was quite unequivocal,
And suffer it I must:

All I know was: she passed me,
Which I did not expect
– And I'd never so craved for
Some crude disrespect.

The Victory

I think it's yours. Furrowing the
Sweat-nights groping for metaphors
– Like the bed's cool patches –
It was hope even then. And other fluences

Carried me somewhere: as, telepathy:
Winging blind wires to carry somehow
News to you. Mad, but it all allowed
The thing to continue. Now, though,

The wires are down. My brain can't ever seem
To stop still enough to think you. My
Bland words talk alone about themselves.
It's yours, this victory, then,

By simple waiting. And, if only you
Might find just what you truly wish through
That same patience – building where
You use it now to reap such disrepair.

Apology for Blasphemy

I can formulate two
Excuses in mitigation:
First, blasphemy surely admits
Some firm, good name:

Only the loved names can
Incite to abuse and treasons:
You cannot blaspheme over what
You must despise.

Second it was, of course,
A trick, in assistance of love,
And no truth. This is the plain fact.
To please a spy,

Huge factories are built
With shuddering walls of dark steel
– Shells of deception, all a lie.
My words did that.

Let an amending tongue
Now penitently cast for means
To rebegin flattery, since
I shrink in fear

Of how I have blasphemed
If nothing can be seen to crack
These literal words; unmake
What they imply.

It is with metaphor
We can assuage, abolish and
Create. I will apologize
With metaphors:

Listen: you could not know,
But when the snow dashed your face, it made
Patterns on white, violent glass, stone-
Scattered; and as

Your mouth just opened, now,
In a slight surprise, all the lions'
Mouths on the bronze financial doors
Dropped their gripped rings.

Eight Investigations

a junction

Not to meet, then. But can't we maintain
One concessionary contact: of
Some meeting in theory – for instance,
Making an agreement to retain
A *kind* of connection by a glance
Each day at some same landmark? Or have

An intersection of routes planned out
On journeys we are often making?
This could be a place where we again
– At quite different times! – could no doubt
'Meet'; (I would cross it like a night train
Crossing points – rapid, darkened, trembling.)

Sprogo (in the Great Belt)

In that sea-stretch, one minor island,
It makes a misty scrap of jutting
Land from wide water. A calmer green
Covers, though, all but one nearly hand-
Wise gesture of cliff, where can be seen
A caged, rusted lantern, cautioning.

You could be compared with any slim,
Chill, passing thing, at will. Yet, the same,
Let me let this dwindling seamark make
Another image: as, on a whim,
Such a quick distant shape could quite take
The diminuendo of your name.

her drawing

No, this Snow Queen (or Cordelia)
Lies drawn, for you, quite differently;
Is merely some unthinking release
Of a moment's work. Still, I see her
As a projection from your own face,
And think: not knowing, you let her be

Like some taller screen image of your
Own contained precision (thus that high
Glance, your own, muting the hands' gestures).
But as she is yours, I must feel
She is truth itself, all such features
Thrown that large by some flattering eye.

second drawing

A kind of swirl of bracken where curve,
Though static, somewhat ambiguous
Symbols, as if grown part of that ground
Of black-stressed, intricate roots (these leave
The surface at no point, but twist round
And upwards into the dubious

Branches of the plant, form letters, signs
Which could mean your name: such as now bring
My mind quite out, away from this sheet,
Elsewhere in time; past these pencilled lines
To their sudden, living start: your neat
Intent smile, your tensed fingers moving).

concession

Privileged now to see you, tell me
(Because I can't know whether I stare
On some frank, actual thing, that skin
Utterly real, or if I yet see
Only a surface which locks me in
With protective, invisible care

As when one looks out at things through glass)
– Are you like somewhere known with plain sight,
Just as clear as you seem? Or do you
Screen off real knowledge, so letting pass
Everything but the quickest key to
That country of air, your clean daylight?

distance

Invent two rings of falling light; wide
For you in the south and the sun's rage,
But not my light – obliged on a neat
Metal table surface to refer
Only to the black words on this sheet:
Chilled, northern light, bronze-shaded. One page

Written already, lies just outside,
In the fawn dusk of the table-edge,
A failure. Still; I can't stop. Be sure
A thousand mere dark miles won't divide
Fact from longing, break down this posture
Of vain love to a better knowledge.

cliffs

Merely thinking up your name in this
Hazardous high strip and ledge in air
Works a consolation: simply that,
Repeating you, any daring is
Practically possible – leant flat
On this shuddering wall, I can stare

Down on the mapped rocks, or out to sea
Unfrightened. Yet in some safe room to
Hear those syllables. . . .The difference
Scares and drowns out all talking for me.
There is no quick courage helps with this
Unexpected way of meeting you.

epistemology

My same eyes once jumped through the page-long
Paragraphs, flickering over such
Banks of abstract words! A *physical*
Power those words had, that caught the strong
Breath of the mind away. The real
Equivalent, now, is your face. Much

That same way your eyes glance this as mine
Glanced; which now face to your forehead's small
Shades and meanings, seek to sublime this
Craving in verbal charts, and refine
Its enigma in a healing verse:
Neurotic; and metaphysical.

Affinity

He. This thing we have, one means by it what starts
Between two people not near to one another
Who have hardly met and never spoken,
Yet know some faint intangible linking
– Neither to be made firm, nor yet to be broken.

She. I don't see it like this at all, but
In opposites: a sudden image of this woman,
Myself, set off on this dark road unaccompanied,
Pacing between blank hedges, her feet
Leaving and reaching echoes, behind and ahead,

And all at once this new thing arriving,
The darkness thinning and varying, the car
Rushing the channels of her ear, its light
Climbing the sides of trees. And her one doubt is to
Ask what *kind* of man he is at the wheel that night

(Is he lover, enemy, casual messenger,
To give all her landscape that white leaping look?)
Since although she cowers back in the mist, bent
In self-protecting fear of what he means,
She has called and craved for . . . this new element.

No Good

It is no good if any man dreams
Her love is attainable by schemes:
No one can win these modern wars,
Why squander tactics on this sort of cause?

It is no good if one decides
Love can be bought, extravagance provides:
She will be right to stay unmoved,
Those won those ways may end unloved.

It is no good, if slyly, one defends
Courses her other lover recommends:
Guile with her is out of place,
She can read any hidden face.

It is no good in the rare state
Of abused purity, the discarnate:
She will think stories, and surmise;
Agree, with pity in her eyes.

It is no good pretending your
Passion is an unbreakable law:
She may obey it! You'll be spent
In some obscene predicament.

It is no good any way one takes,
The sin is travel if roads are mistakes,
The plague is feet if it's no good proceeding:
I do not think this is too misleading.

ALAN BROWNJOHN

A Few Syllabics

You said you couldn't
Do other. You were
That conventional
You just walked 'into
The night.' It hurled rain.

They had left on the
Light in the builders'
Yard to stop burglars,
And you had eight wet
Miles' ride. But what was

Not usual was (and
I didn't know) you
Carried a man's child
Two months uninter-
rupted away in

You. It wasn't mine,
I loved you, and by
This bit of chance, your
Not telling me, you
Left, to take her on

Till birth, and to push
Her onwards down time
To stand here (a child
Two months in her too,
Which I do know, and

The new child not mine
Either) where the light
Left on in that yard
Again shows me that
Shape I love, as we

Look at your photo
She holds (bit of chance!)
And I wonder if,
After all these dark
Things, I'll let *her* leave.

Sunsets

Suddenly caught by how it seems
Possible and quite credible that,
In this last windless minute at

Sunset, that downspread of fields I watch
(Gazing past, from this vantage hill,
Just visible cows to the town) will

Have darkened a little – even though
You can't measure this, and it may be
Your eyes don't tell it truthfully –

I sense a comparison with
Some points in the progress of love:
Times when each element *has* to move

At just the stage when you would want
It at rest – when, dispassionate
-ly, you would want to define and state

To yourself just where you stand. It may
Be a simple error to believe
That love runs on like that, you can deceive

Yourself quite easily. But
So often love seems to be set
On rushing you past anywhere you get

A chance to arrest it, and talk.
And in this, as with nightfall, you sense
That you cannot make much pretence

Of defying any darkness.
It leaves you no other choice.
It happens in front of your eyes.

The Space

Then why see it? This 'flat and ample
Space over which you walk at no one angle,
Led as by something very like your will?'

You could go on with proper concerns. You
Are boiling tea, typing some letter, listening
To politics when it comes. Why let it, why let

It come? – That pale, clean stretch
Stays small, and won't usurp the whole. So
I let it come. There is no harmful freedom.

But where do you go across that space? Do you
See things, see anyone? I don't go anywhere
But across it; taut and clear, though the wind leans at me.

Further, it might be a world, and not safe:
It might be stayed in. I keep it unfulfilled.
Its colour? Certain shadows, shades of green.

– And whoever she who walks there, and stands,
She won't tremble into definition, isn't
Like Fournier's girl, say, on the steps and real.

Then why let it come at all? Only that, to this
All common facts yearn to approximate,
While time strains to reach it. And it

Won't be otherwise, it refuses, and must
Return as plainly as before; nothing but
A kind of sober walking-space. – I see

You are not answered why, nor sense why I let it come.

Two Songs

(HOMAGE TO LOUIS MACNEICE)

1

Tug out one snapping knot into flat string
And tie a new one
Pull out two paper-clips straight
And re-bend them
Let only your mirror weep

Cut three potatoes through
But hold the halves together
Break four white saucers along cracks
And glue the pieces
Let only your mirror weep

Shake out five plain, clean sheets
And refold them
Tear six new scarves across
Then sew them whole
Let only your mirror weep

Wrench out seven firm locks
But fix back the jarred metals
Smash through eight wide windows
And cellophane the spaces
Let only your mirror weep

Walk a razed block round nine times
Aching for buildings
Refer to your death on ten occasions
And let the word die into silence
Let only your mirror weep

2

The pheasants rightangle away into the thicket;
The mill sails appear on the right, as the map ventures;
The sedge bends to the light wind politely, not constrained;
I love you as detail.

The church has a tower the miniature of its tower;
Finished sacks, thrown down, glitter and litter on the field;
Three day-owls scatter towards the approaching wood;
I love you for detail.

The lane turns into two ruts with a thick grass centre;
Rides of pines come thinly down to entreat at the hedge;
Hay-blocks provide for the month under polythene sheets;
I love you in detail.

Turned soil rests and waits in the damp, clean and unharried;
The concealing flat cloud glows, in foreground to the sun;
One gust flicks beads of wet from the grass at crazed angles;
I love you through detail.

A 202

This coarse road, my road, struggles out
South-east across London, an exhausted
Grey zigzag of stubborn, unassimilable
    Macadam, passing hoardings pasted

With blow-ups of cricket journalists, blackened
And not-quite-Georgian terraces,
Shagged-out Greens of geraniums and
    Floral coats-of-arms, lost pieces

Of genteel façade behind and above
Lyons' shopfronts and 'Pullum Promotions',
– Journeying between wired-off bombed lots glossy
    With parked Consuls, making diversions

Round bus depots and draggled estates
In circumlocutory One Ways,
Netting aquaria in crammed pet store windows,
    Skirting multi-racial bingo queues,

And acquiring, for its self-hating hoard, old black-railed
Underground bogs advising the Seamen's Hospital,
'Do-It-Yourself' shops, 'Funerals and Monuments', and
    Victorian Charrington pubs. All

Along its length it despoils, in turn, a sequence
Of echoless names: Camberwell, Peckham,
New Cross Gate; places having no recorded past
    Except in histories of the tram.

It takes out, in cars, arterial affluence
At week-ends, returning it as bad blood

To Monday mornings in town. It is altogether
  Like a vein travelled by hardy diseases, an aged

Canal dredgeable for bodies left behind
On its soulless travels: Sixty-Nine,
Thirty-Six, One-Eight-Five. It takes no clear
  Attitude anyone could easily define

So as to resist or admire it. It seems to hate you
Possessively, want to envelop you in nothing
Distinguishable or distinguished, like its own
  Smothered slopes and rotting

Valleys. This road, generally, is one for
The long-defeated; and turns any ironic
Observer's tracer-isotope of ecology,
  Sociology or hopeful manic

Verse into a kind of mere
Nosing virus itself. It leaves its despondent, foul
And intractable deposit on its own
  Banks all the way like virtually all

Large rivers, particularly the holy ones, which it
Is not. It sees little that deserves to be undespised.
It only means well in the worst of ways.
  How much of love is much less compromised?

Winter Appointment

Now, after too long,
A fool's courage flows back again, and assists me
To the dentist's chair and his unheavenly lights.

The vanished space between me and this house has been
Like the gap scaring
Some anxious lover and all that he dared not risk.

Horse, hawk and debutante in the smooth magazines
Soothe, in the waiting-room, me, with tired coat and grey
Mouth. Rising, I think:

Scales of sharp justice
Appear to be carefully balancing this out:
For those gropings at pleasure, this payment of pain.

Two weeks gone since my first daring venture, when I
Knew he would not start
And I only need fearfully submit to that

Quick, sinister, flicking parade of the wan street
Of my mouth, that tilting of searching mirrors, prods
At each drab structure,

Surveyor's verdict:
No site to be cleared, or buildings to be shored up,
Though some cleaning, for appearances, would improve.

But! – *I'll take a small X-ray of that one, in case . . .*
And two weeks of fright
Till today's visit, even if swift certainty

Soon now. (Yes. . . .Take a large X-ray of Diana,
I'd still not quite know what meant reassurance and
What, shaking terror.)

So. Today's the day. . . .
Well, I *could* have shirked it. . . .What more helpful than to
Put off yet another painful self-attrition?

Do sit. Bleak time of revealing: no comfort here.
A train grates, roars down
The cutting outside, the smooth cat flops off the sill.

Something will have to be done. . .You see, there was this
Shadow like a sin I didn't think I might have
On the X-ray plate.

Nothing but to *sit*
As the cotton wool dabs at the affronted gums
And his white arm slopes to the swivel tray. But – please –

Talk, please – Rhodesia, anything – till the
Injection takes. . . . I'll
Lie open-mouthed at the honour of van der Byl.

A sort-of napkin fitted below my neck. 'Not
Where he eats, but where. . . .' (Diana-pray-grace-this-meal-
Before-and-during!)

. . .Christ! Anything *must*
Be painful to be salutary. His foot pumps
The chair close (think of her, think of her, think of her,

Seize her presence with some poet's metaphysical
Calling of her to
This moment: for example, though he be a man,

I'll allow Diana to visit the dentist:
His drill is the one of all the violations
Which purges and mends.)

Jarring suddenness;
Intermission; recommencement. *Take a good rinse.*
We are come now, I would say, to the nub of this...

Pain accurately descends his cold, angled crane
Of quivering wires:
Bleak hysteria of the burr changing its note.

* * *

And how long do these renewals last? What hopes place
In his painful skill, or in any curative
Promise I might have?

There are no answers;
Except to make a quick leap in equivocal
Relief and faith from his chair, and, to myself, say

That to have no trust
In teeth mended, or promises, helps no raw nerve....
A cavity clear, metal could firm in the space.

A sure, pure flame melted his amalgam. At last
He has carved a surface, he has stripped that napkin
Away; so I rise,

Convinced. With ball-point
I fray his dotted line, sense comfort in the gift
Of this restored street in hopeful mid-afternoon,

Down which Diana
Could be ready softly to walk, as down some now –
Cleansed and part-shuttered Piccadilly, quite alone.

Incident on 6th August

Last and most hurting stroke of the wide,
Inescapable sunlight, a flash from some turning car's
windscreen
Streaks across to my eyes and blots the whole day black.

I walk on looking out through a pulsing cloud
At the disfigured street, planting a
Seething blur on every face and dress:

They move, half-black and writhing, towards me,
Not knowing, in their late afternoon. They
Are talking and smiling and conducting their

Own concerns beneath my surface of wounds. And
Who am I to tell them they are
Scorched blotches in an insane ignorance?

They would think me the mad one.

Old Company

What is there underneath this tight and
Scarlet creasing at their eye-corners,
As the mouth-stretching laughter-spasm holds
And stacks each man's entire, shuddering
Body on top of his stomach folds?

Their faces seize in this concerted anguish.
The spread-out, cumbersome limbs around the circle
Look like helpless pain to possess.
But they will laugh, and stay. Their risen steam
Muffles each window, hides the street's greyness.

Gregarious mankind.... Old company
Can ride down any fear as the stale
Seconds of their present unendurably tear
Them piecemeal away from those fresher
Seconds of their mutual past, where

The first laugh started. Each one's ageing face
Makes now a shield for his flesh, here where
All shields grip together grimacing
On phalanx-night against the terror
In one expressionless, unchanging thing.

Hedonist

It was not the religious pleasure-principle,
The supposed, long quest of the libertine; nor
Was it any kind of arrant desire for
Immolation in some seizing mode of brief
Forgetfulness. It was no sort of strained belief,
Or meditated act; but much more simple:

It was the sense of the sufficient good-ness
Of the next thing beyond the present thing:
The food after a day not eating,
The landing after the stairs, the prospect of some
Prospect filling the ten next minutes, should they come.
It was sleep; sometimes. But simpler even than these,

It could be just the sunlight, as an amiable event
To walk out into from the thick
Complexities of his room, leaving cigarettes, stick
And tablets and trusting, for once,
To his own feet and the friendliness of distance,
And to mere walking alone on the bright pavement.

Of Consequence

Before James Carra knew Anne Furlington
She made love, often, the first in both their lives,
Under a slipping mauve quilt in a seaport,
With nightlong traffic noise disturbing;
There being wallpaper the same as in her
College room; and it was Peter Daines.
It was the world. No one seemed later hurt, or
Finally betrayed.
                It was not of consequence.

When Hester Lang told Cavan Benther that
Hidden in some long spell away from him was
A week when Philip Quernier was prepared
And it happened three times (but each time one of them
Pretended) an hour was enough for Cavan's
Fury. Nor were these people heartless. It was
Not of consequence. Such oddness at such distance
Could be healed.
                It was the world.

Elizabeth Pender felt that past could be
Contentedly left as past concerning
William Stennett's beds where Margaret Bourn
Fought conscience and hindering fear. She
Only nodded; and thought. Such guileless frankness
Gave a lot of help. This would leave
No injury-traces. . . . It was the world. In minutes
Their hands came coolly together.
                It was not of consequence.

For My Son

Not ever to talk when merely requested,
Not ever to be the performing child,
This is what you would establish;
                                        always keeping
Private and awkward counsel against
All coaxing; and going – one hopes –
The way of a good will,

To your own true designs. Which is
The way of some human institutions,
Growing not as any collective urge
                                    would have them
(In its own placable image) but into
Their own more wayward value – strong,
Untidy, original, self-possessed.

Breaking Eggs

It is as if she chose to exist
To scathe forgiveable sins
– In which she could be right;

But to watch her way, for example,
With pardonable pride, or any faintly
False dignity or ceremoniousness

Is somehow terrible.
And to prepare a meal
(Though no one should dare to asperse her skill),
She will unclasp each poised, mature

Vegetable's grip upon itself, leaf
By pathetic leaf, intently; or crack
The fragile and decorous eggs

With rapid and curt fingers, not smiling.
It would look like no more than cold spite
If it were not her own kind of care; and

If she could not also, with a mere knife only,
Take up (precise and chilling miracle!)
Each omelette into surging fabric-folds.

KAO U888

What we pursue pursues us,
We are such rich quarries for
Our own energies; and the long hunt hunts
Us.

Kent Archive Office, Robert Garrett:
Forbears in the Thanet Cavalry,
A squirearchic family, a ducal marriage,
Promotion aspiring to him in
Peninsular places. The fiancé's letters
Are the ladder mounting him, Imperial wars
Wage him.

He elevates money to officer-status.
How perfectly Portugal offers
Convenient insolence to be kicked downstairs!

Oh, easy it must have been, to be
Worked by instinct through wealthy alliances, to
The division in the Crimea, to
That Adjutant-Generalship....

Why choose this example?
It distances.
It detaches.
I am not its exact equivalent.

It's just that it's like
Any path of honourable ruin and delusion
Paving itself for the walker in pride,
Flattering his feet with challenging distances.

The Clouds

The craftsmen in my line bred out.
I drive, but could I mend a fuse.
My fathers handled founts of words
My brain would catch and fingers lose.

I find a fair excuse, to serve:
There has, in our society,
Been 'social change', which makes these skills
Much less of a necessity.

Beyond your shoulder I can see
A saucer – stamped out by machine –
On the formica shelf near where
We lie on quilts of terylene.

No sort of ancient expertise
Goes to create these modern things:
To them, no craftsman's hand its pride
Or love for their completeness brings.

Their very make and feel rejects
Any thought that such loving powers
Nurtured their shapes to what they are
Through someone's calm and patient hours.

That care seems obsolete – Yes, I know
You were your parents' artefact,
Your perfect head, shoulders and back
Made in a sort-of skilful act.

But when I move a careful hand
(No craftsman's art its legacy)

And dot a pattering line to count
Your poised and tensing vertebrae

It's not *great* numeracy I want,
Or flair for cold technologies
– Such details are not wanted in
All kinds of loving enterprise.

Nor do we need such skills to lose
All sense of this room, house and street . . .
And don't doubt, though we use no craft,
That love it is makes this complete.

– And, well, on looking up I see,
As a sweet end to summer's drought,
Some wholly unskilled clouds which pour
Blessings of rain on Barons Court.

MICHAEL HAMBURGER

A Poet's Progress

Like snooker balls thrown on the table's faded green,
Rare ivory and weighted with his best ambitions,
At first his words are launched: not certain what they mean,
He loves to see them roll, rebound, assume positions
Which – since not he – some higher power has assigned.
But now the game begins: dead players, living critics
Are watching him – and suddenly one eye goes blind,
The hand that holds the cue shakes like a paralytic's,
Till every thudding, every clinking sound portends
New failure, new defeat. Amazed, he finds that still
It is not he who guides his missiles to their ends
But an unkind geometry that mocks his will.

If he persists, for years he'll practise patiently,
Lock all the doors, learn all the tricks, keep noises out,
Though he may pick a ghost or two for company
Or pierce the room's inhuman silence with a shout.
More often silence wins: then soon the green felt seems
An evil playground, lawless, lost to time, forsaken,
And he a fool caught in the water weeds of dreams,
Whom only death or frantic effort can awaken.

At last, a master player, he can face applause,
Looks for a fit opponent, former friends, emerges;
But no one knows him now. He questions his own cause
And has forgotten why he yielded to those urges,
Took up a wooden cue to strike a coloured ball.
Wise now, he goes on playing; both his house and heart
Unguarded solitudes, hospitable to all
Who can endure the cold intensity of art.

Paddington Canal

A mocking mirror, the black water turns
Tall houses upside down, makes learned men
Walk on their heads in squares of burning light;
Lovers like folded bats hang in a kiss,
Swaying as if a breeze could sever them.
The barges, giant sea-birds fast asleep,
Lie on the surface, moored and motionless;
Then, drowning gently, are drawn down to join
The sunken lovers and the acrobats.
Out of the grim dimensions of a street
Slowly I see another landscape grow
Downwards into a lost reality;
A magic mirror, the black water tells
Of a reversed Atlantis wisely built
To catch and to transform
The wasted substance of our daily acts,
Accommodate our mad and lovely doubles
In a more graceful city timelessly.

From the Note-Book of a European Tramp

IV

Sun and snow; yet in my head
Town thoughts, street griefs revolve,
Problems which I did not solve
When I was tame and led
A domesticated life,
Read the papers and could
Not guess that ever I should
Eat with a pocket-knife.

Mid-February; but here
Winter drips from the trees;
Higher up small boys on skis,
Virtuosi of fear,
Embody the unborn spring
That gives them mastery.
Surely my mind should not be
Bothered with anything.

Moon and snow; I am the same
Poor fool who maunders down
Every street of every town
And does not need a name,
Since the arc-lights cast a sheen
Not clear enough to trace
Much more than a basic face,
Eyes that seek the unseen.

IX

That the creative mind might rest and trees
Might flatter it like household grenadiers,
The pride of kings besieged by mortal fears

Planned gardens as impeccable as these;
Caserta, Schoenbrunn, Sanssouci, Versailles:
The water canalized, strict symmetry
Of column, statue, path, periphery,
Bounded but boundless to the scanning eye.

Till truant flowers and weeds like dancing fauns
Broke through that sterile stillness and cried out;
Soon sandwich wrappings blossomed on the lawns.
The tortured tourist came and lounged about;
But from that Eden built for Adams dead,
Eves obsolete, even the dream had fled.

XI

The townsman on his yielding bed
Thinks that the world will end when he
On the bare floorboards lies instead.
He also who was forced to see
The mind's own mattresses ripped up
And many a recipient head
Smashed like a saucer or a cup
Feels that by rights he should be dead.

True, there are moments when he finds
That metaphysics was no more
Than luxury of idle minds,
Soft padding round a rotten core –
Particularly in the Spring
When Chaos, ever young, unbinds
Gods who are game for anything
And demi-gods of various kinds.

In winter, though he's far from sure.
He says his prayers just in case
A word in the right place might cure
His pangs, redeem all men's disgrace;
And still it seems a little weird
That the earth's axle is secure
When all the nightmares he most feared
Prosper in daylight and endure.

Lines on Brueghel's Icarus

The ploughman ploughs, the fisherman dreams of fish;
Aloft, the sailor through a world of ropes
Guides tangled meditations, feverish
With memories of girls forsaken, hopes
Of brief reunions, new discoveries,
Past rum consumed, rum promised, rum potential.
Sheep crop the grass, lift up their heads and gaze
Into a sheepish present: the essential,
Illimitable juiciness of things,
Greens, yellows, browns are what they see.
Churlish and slow, the shepherd, hearing wings –
Perhaps an eagle's – gapes uncertainly.

Too late. The worst had happened: lost to man
The angel, Icarus, for ever failed,
Fallen with melted wings when, near the sun
He scorned the ordering planet, which prevailed
And, jeering, now slinks off, to rise once more.
But he – his damaged purpose drags him down –
Too far from his half-brothers on the shore,
Hardly conceivable, is left to drown.

A Brief Biography

This poor amphibian on the dry land of prose
Watched others labour; now hoped to emulate
The troubled ant who, gathering details, goes
Patiently about his business, to create;
Now sickened by the sight, he envied fish –
Whose yielding element, it seemed, fulfilled
Their faintest, mute unformulated wish
Lest impulse should grow weak by being willed –
For foolishly, deliciously intent
On self-expression, all day long they played
In the clear liquid of abandonment,
Poetic palaces of light and shade . . .
Then with the ducks became identified,
Domestic, democratic, sociable,
Not over-clean, but innocent of pride,
Products of humble homesteads and the Fall . . .
Till he saw swans – a pair of them – and knew;
Art is aristocratic. Lend me pure white
To glide on time's calm waters or in the blue
Expanse of summer answer the infinite!

Oh, he was none of these; could scarcely swim,
Not walk at all, nor fly, nor work, nor play.
What most he loved most cruelly wounded him
By being loveliest when he turned away.
He could sit still for hours, catch a few flies –
A modest minimum – on his floating log,
But soon would languish for the great surprise,
Proof that he was not what he was, a frog.

Ants climbed and stumbled, fell and climbed once more,
The leisured fishes glittered in glassy streams,

Ducks paddled, dived or waddled on the shore,
The swans, two distant lovers, guarded their dreams.
He gazed and hoped and envied, rarely tried,
Yet, always changing, giddily revolved,
Restless till in the unremembering tide
His tortured multiplicity dissolved.

In October

In October the pregnant woman walked by the river
When autumn's failing green on the water's face
Conjures a world without depth, a landscape of glass.
She saw leaves and their images meet and saw them severed,
From the tall trees, glowing, a flicker of red fall down,
Leaves of the weeping willows drop and drown,
Cracking that mirror of green, the immaculate water.
'Tears of time,' she thought; 'O my son or daughter
Due to be born with the lambs and, like them, slaughtered
By the sudden thrust in war, slow waste in peace,
To wonder, to hope for a while, then glimmer passionless.
Man's grief I perpetuate, which else would cease.'

Faint, but golden, the sun broke through the haze;
She saw dead leaves assembled on the river's bed,
Water-weeds groping for food, their green unshed,
And above, new buds, minute, on the naked boughs.
'Nameless you are,' she thought, 'my son or daughter,
Nameless as unborn leaves, dead leaves and the water,
A particle, passing but blessed, between always and never.
Man's joy I perpetuate, the tree and the river,
Summer's unbroken mirror, the cracking glass
And the stillness that spreads where leaf and image divide.'

The Dual Site

To my twin who lives in a cruel country
  I wrote a letter at last;
For my bones creaked out in our long silence
  That seven years had passed,

Seven whole years since he and I
  By word or token exchanged
The message I dare not do without:
  That still we are not estranged,

Though I watch figures in a city office
  And he the waves of the sea,
Keeping no count since he hardly cares
  What happens to him or to me;

Since to names and numbers he closed his head
  When, children still, we were parted,
Chose birth and death for his calendar,
  But leaves the dates uncharted,

Being one who forgets what I remember,
  Who knows what I do not,
Who has learnt the ways of otter and raven
  While I've grown polyglot.

Lately I found a cactus in flower
  And feared for his apple-trees,
Dozed in the club and saw his cattle
  Drag with a foul disease,

And my bones grown stiff with leaning and lying
  Cried out that I'll labour in vain
Till I help my twin to rebuild his hovel
  That's open to wind and rain.

So I sent him a note, expecting no answer,
  And a cheque he'd never cash,
For I knew he was one who'd smile if he heard
  His own roof come down with a crash,

But above the porpoise-leaping bay
  Where ploughshare fin and tail
Cut furrows the foam-flecked sea fills up
  He'd stand in the swishing gale,

Calm as the jackdaws that nest in crannies
  And no more prone to doubt,
With gull and cormorant perched on the rocks
  Would wait the weather out.

Yet he wrote by return: 'Have no fear for your dwelling
  Though dry-rot gnaws at the floors;
Only lighten their load of marble and metal,
  Keep clear the corridors,

Move out the clocks that clutter your study,
  And the years will leave you alone:
Every frame I know of lasts long enough,
  Though but cardboard, wood or bone.

And spare me your nightmares, brother, I beg you,
  They make my daemons laugh,
They scare the spirits that rarely will visit
  A man with no wand or staff,

With no symbol, no book and no formula,
  No lore to aid him at all,
Who wherever he walks must find the image
  That holds his mentors in thrall.

But your waking cares put down on paper
  For me to give to the wind
That the seed may fall and the dry leaf crumble,
  Not a wisp be left behind

Of the tangle that hides the dual site
  Where even you and I
Still may meet again and together build
  One house before we die.'

Emblem

Only for love of love
High up this hunter shot
And missed the snow-white dove.

Then, descending to the plain,
Entered a pitch-black wood
And, blindly, shot again.

For the sake of the dove, of mountain sunlight and snow
Deep in dark woods he seeks a wounded doe.

Epitaph for a Horseman

Let no one mourn his mount, upholstered bone
He rode so cruelly over bog and stone,
Log, fence and ditch in every kind of weather;
Nor glibly hint those two came down together:
A horse fell dead and cast his master down,
But by that fall their union was undone.
A broken jade we found, the rider gone,
Leaving no token but his cold clean gear,
Bit, reins and riding-crop for friends to gather.
None but a beast's remains lie buried here.

Blind Man

He can hear the owl's flight in daylight
When, surprised, on silky wings it shoots
From a low perch; and by the open window at night
The stag-beetles blundering in the hedges
On the far side of the meadow. Geese half a mile away
Honk near as hooters of swerving cars
And do not alarm him. Indifferently he awaits
Dogs that he feared when they slunk or bounded
Visible at him, as if in his carapace
Of darkness for ever secure from harm,
Wombed and housed and coffined within a wound
That has hardened to armour. The screech and the hum
Blend and subside in a resonant quiet,
Shapes he has fumbled to feel fall back
Into unbroken space when his hands forget them,
And still are present in his no man's land;
Above the nightmare tamed by light's extinction
The apple that hangs unplucked, grown fabulous.

Conformist

Branded in childhood, for thirty years he strove
To hide the scar, and truly to believe
In the true fundaments of that commonweal
Which once had outlawed him beyond repeal,
And with true awe, true gratitude, true love
Would gaze upon the incorruptible guard
Before the gate – the keeper of his peace
Who in mean streets could live anonymous . . .

Until conformity brought its reward:
A crested, gilt-edged card. The great gate opened,
A pair of stiff lips cracked and let him pass
Into those halls his half life's dreams had deepened;

And out again . . . to breathe the ownerless air,
Night sky transfigured, lucent, fresh and clear
After the ceilings puffed in emulation.
His own place found at last; his own self found –
Outside, outside – his heritage regained
By grace of exile, of expropriation.

What had he seen, ushered behind the gate?
The dress and furniture of his own terrors,
A glittering medal pinned on his own wound,
And, at the heart, an empty hall of mirrors.

Healed now, of health, unmasked, of honesty,
In, out again he passed, with one smile met
The questioning eyes of flunkey, potentate,
Townsman and guard shrunk to complicity,

All one to him at one with every station
Since none was his, nor ever now could be;
Come late into the freedom his from birth,
To breathe the air, and walk the ownerless earth.

A Horse's Eye

I did not stop today at the five-barred gate,
Did not wait for the old white draught-horse at grass,
Unshod, unharnessed these many years; walked past,
Preocicuped, but something made me look back:
Her head was above the gate, her neck was straight,
But I caught her eye, a wicked, reproachful look
From one small eye slanted in my direction.
What right, I defied the old mare, what right had she
To expect caresses, the grass foolishly plucked
For her hanging lip, her yellow, broken teeth,
And her great historical belly? Of course she's a relic
Curious now as the old white country house
That stood empty and alluring in the wood behind her
Till converted into flats – not as useless as she,
Who will never become a tractor! What farmer would care?
Only some town-bred, animist, anthropomorphic rambler
Or week-end motorist looking for what he's lost.

I walked on; but plainly her glance had spoken to me,
As an old peasant's might in a foreign country
Communicating neither words nor thought, but the knowledge
Of flesh that has suffered labour in rain and wind,
Fed, relaxed, enjoyed and opposed every season.
Broken now. Close to death. And how differently broken
From that Cossack mare the clumsiest rider could sit,
All speed and nerve and power that somehow responded
To the faintest twitch of a will less tense than her own!
Wild nature still; her eye no peasant's eye,
But lava under glass, tellurian fire contained.

As for the old white mare, her reproach was just:
Because she was too intelligible I had passed her by,
Because not alien enough, but broken as men are broken;
Because the old white house was converted now,
The wood about to be felled, a tractor chugging
Beyond the hill, and awkwardly she trotted
On legs too thin for her belly bloated with age,
Alone in her meadow, at grass, and close to death.

Tides

To wake without fail when milk bottles shake in
  their racks,
Scrape one's face in the morning, every morning,
Take the same route to work and say 'good morning'
To the same row of scraped or powdered faces –
I cursed the roundness of this earth, I raged
At every self-perpetuating motion,
Hated the sea, that basher of dumb rock,
For all her factory of weeds and fishes,
The thumps, the thuds, the great reverberations –
Too much in rhythm; jarring, but by rote.

The metronome it was in my own head
That ticked and ticked; caged cricket in my head
That chirped and chirped until I had no ear
For syncopation, counterpoint of stillness
Beating against all music – of the sea,
Of birds and men, of season and machine,
Even of cricket and of metronome.
In silence I learned to listen; in the dark to look.

And unrepeatable now each morning's light
Modulates, shuffles, probes the daily faces
Often too suddenly different, like the street,
This weathered wall re-pointed, that new one cracked,
Apple trees that I prune while I forget
The shape of last year's boughs, cankered or grown,
And where that stump is, one that died in blossom;
Forget the hill's curve under the aerial masts.

No, wheels, grind on; seasons, repeat yourselves;
Milk bottles, rattle; familiars, gabble 'good morning';

Breed, hatch, digest your weeds and fishes, sea,
Omit no beat, nor rise to tidal waves.
Various enough the silences cut in
Between the rock cave's boom and the small
wader's cry.

Old Poacher

Learned in woods
As troubadour in words
Delicate as a troubadour's lady,
Killer of does grown doe-like
In nostril, ear,
Lithely, gravely he stalks
His quarry
That will never know death.
And men stalk him.

Only a hawk cries
Above the clearing;
Robin and blackbird are still.
It is the hawk will cry
Till his eye meets
The man's eye
And silent he dips over oak-tops
In flight that is not fear
But hunger's cunning.

Fearless, wily, the man
Listens:
For dog's pad on moss, dry leaves,
Brushed fern, torn bramble,
Panting breath, cough,
Squelch of boot in trough;
Or cropped grass,
Nibble on low hazel bough,
Scuttle of hoof, claw.

And feels again
The thorny joy

Of his great indifference;
To have almost forgotten death
In the woods, in hunger's
Mastery over fear;
With senses grown
Reliable, reliant,
And a man's mind
To savour the sense –
Hunting, hunted, both hawk and deer.

Security

1

So he's got there at last, been received as a partner –
In a firm going bankrupt;
Found the right place (walled garden) arranged for a
  mortgage –
But they're pulling the house down
To make room for traffic.
Worse winds are rising. He takes out new policies
For his furniture, for his life,
At a higher premium
Against more limited risks.

2

Who can face the winds, till the panes crack in their frames?
And if a man faced them, what in the end could he do
But look for shelter like all the rest?
The winds too are afraid, and blow from fear.

3

I hear my children at play
And recall that one branch of the elm-tree looks dead;
Also that twenty years ago now I could have been parchment
Cured and stretched for a lampshade,
Who now have children, a lampshade
And the fear of those winds.

4

I saw off the elm-tree branch
To find that the wood was sound;
Mend the fences yet again,
Knowing they'll keep out no one,
Let alone the winds.
For still my children play,
And shall tomorrow, if the weather holds.

After Attica

I

Rock, rock and the sea.
Fishermen mending their nets
In the shade of tall houses
Locked up when the captains died out,
Galaxidi fell silent,
The olive trade passed it by.

At Itea now
The great barrels are filled,
The ferries loaded with strangers.
And Itea's fishermen sit
In the shade of low hovels
Mending their nets.

2

Three vultures glide
Towards Parnassos
From the olive grove of Amphissa;
Over temple, theatre, stadium,
And the pine groves above.

The flycatcher flits
From fallen pediment
To mended pillar.
A long brown snake
Darts from loose rubble
To rooted thyme.
The holy site is a garden
For goldfinch, marigold, orchis.

Three vultures glide down
Over the valley

Where hooded crows
Perch on judas trees
To snatch the larger share.
Broken cry
Of a donkey laden with branches.
A shepherd stands in the glare,
Whistles to bell-wether, ewe,
And the lambs will follow.

Soon melted snow
Will replenish the little river
That now is an ochre track;
The swelling asphodel bulb
Will be celebrated
And, after fasting, the slaughtered lamb.
There will be dancing,
To Giorgios the barber's guitar,
Neither child nor mule will be beaten
Till the women resume
Their digging, pruning, picking
That the ritual may be fulfilled.

The god who came from the sun
Has returned to the sun.
The prophetess is a cave.
The Castalian spring
Waters almond and fig tree.

The words to the song have changed.
This terrace carved out of rock
Bore a shrine, a villa, a pillbox:
Anemones bend in the breeze,
And three yellow vultures ride it
Back to the sea.

3

In halflight
Heavy with incense
Eyes blink
At unblinking eyes,
Black symmetry
Against a heaven of gold.
King's gown and shepherd's kirtle,
Green, red and blue
Pay homage to black.
Amplified in the domed silence
The humming of bees.

Scarred by earthquake, war,
Patched and impoverished
The forecourt collects
Larger quietness
Of mountains and valley.
Heavier than incense
The fragrance of blossoming laurel.
From a shallow basin's rim
Bees drink the cold spring water.
A monk on the balcony
Reads yesterday's paper.

DEMONSTRATION IN ATHENS –
Truncheon, tear gas turned
On women, old men.
Survivors perhaps,
Defenders once of these vineyards
When three hundred were rounded up,
Herded into the shambles
To pay for one soldier's death.

And now the tourists:
A café here, a shop,
Rugs from Aráchova,
Mementoes of places missed out
Or blankly visited,
Works of art – too many –
Conceived in the camera's womb,
Undeveloped, unborn,
Their guidebooks that leap
From Oedipus at the crossroads
To our holy Luke,
Neither mention or name those others.

So we moved our ikons
To a homely chapel,
Left to them the basilica,
Open now, and empty
Till the next coach pulls up
With click of shutters, buzz
Not of bees, but voices
Complaining of roads and hotels.

Pray for them,
Pray for eyes that blink
At unblinking eyes,
Outgazed, like us all.
That ceiling too will go
Despite our propping, patching;
May there be eyes here to blink
At the sun
And be outgazed,
Hands to water lettuce,
To tend the bees.

The Road

It begins near Venice
A Venice of chasms and pools,
And above a coastline longer than vision,
Gently curves
Into a south or east without end.
Always the question is
How far can I walk it
Across what frontiers
Into what vastnesses,
More golden mist,
Woods ever denser, darker,
Mountains more mountainous
Above a more dazzling sea.

Always I am detained;
As by this new nation
Of displaced persons
Who are rarely visited,
Whose nationhood is a cause.
They needed me,
Appealed to my fellowship,
Involved me in schemes,
Charged me with missions
To friends whom I never reached.

If only I could move on
To the wilder, more alien countries
Farther along the road.

The Search

As commanded, I looked for my origin,
Passed through the town in which my grandfather settled
And found no street that I knew;
On through the suburbs, blind bungalows,
Lilac, laburnum, narrowly flowering
And out into mountains, woods,
Far provinces, infinities of green.
Walked, walked, by day, by night,
Always sure of the route
Though the people grew foreign, bizarre;
And the birds, a species unheard of, remembered me.

At last I came to a village
Where they told me: here you were born.
An unlikely place – no petrol pump, office block, poster? –
Yet I could not deny it, and asked them the name:
Why, Mors, need we tell you, m o r s, MORS.

Scenario

1

He came home. Came home? The house
Did not fit the garden, the view.
Their own, locked up in his absence?
Another she'd bought and unlocked?
On the floor of a half-lit room
Lay family silver, baskets full,
Tapestries, paintings he could not remember possessing,
A screen of beaten brass,
Concertina of Indian dancers,
Flimsy, garish, in half-relief,
All dumped there to be discarded
Or, if he chose, kept to furnish the house.

2

Threading his way to the garden through crowds of guests
He looked for his landmarks and frontiers:
To the north a great railway station
Linked to the house by a concrete road
That brought more guests in taxis.
To the south a valley and, hazily shining,
Cupolas, palace roofs, towers
Framed in mountain-tops, wooded ravines.

A woman stood near him, a stranger.
'Lend me your eyes,' he begged her, 'I mean,
Tell me, describe what *you* see.
My left eye fear, my right eye desire
Will not focus; all shifts and blurs.
Where am I?' She laughed, and moved on.

3

Room after room. Bare galleries, halls,
Passages, thronged with guests.
Unrecognized he explored them,
Came to an improvised kitchen
And found his wife with a man.
'Hallo,' she said, and smoothed her lover's hair.
He turned on his heel, strode through the staring crowds
And, alone in the garden, waited.
They followed: a burly man,
A fence between them. He vaulted,
The man seized his leg, pulled him down,
Hurled a knife, then a pitchfork,
But felled by his fists, lay still.

The single boom of a gong.

4

Longer than sight the table stretched,
Between bare walls without end,
Faces, faces, to each of which now with an effort
He could have attached a name, a function, a place.
'So the three of you will be living together'
Neighed the sleek-haired one with the bow tie.
'It's hard enough to live with one's wife,
Let alone her lover' he heard himself answer.

A *bon mot* apparently. Between their guffaws
He corrected himself: 'But no reflection
On *my* wife. A general observation.'
Had she heard him? He did not know where she was.

5

He walked with her and their only child, a daughter,
No house in sight, no intruder,
The three of them anywhere, walking in silence.
He turned to her: 'Is it true . . .?'
Needing her confirmation of the silence
That made her true again, gathered into a moment
Their moments and years.
'Quiet' she said, 'not now – the child'
And knifeblade, pitchfork went home,
Pierced him with love, the first and the last pain.

For No One

So we meet again, little girl
Whose blue eyes taught me
How to say nothing, to look
And be merged in looking.
I saw you there and I listened,
But you cannot hear me,
Nor do I know where you are.
No need, in that place
Where to look is enough,
Where to meet is a marriage
Nowhere, for ever,
Nothing can be undone.
Here, I should have passed by, unrecognizing,
You a woman now, still young but not beautiful,
With a bad complexion. But Beatrice was your name,
Recalled to me without words though your eyes were not
  even blue
And now you chattered gaily about yourself,
About living from hand to mouth, luxuriously.
Because you were Beatrice, nothing had changed between us;
Because nothing had changed between us, I knew your name.

Memory

My wives do not write.
Sweetly young, hair flowing,
They walk where they belong,
Riverside, lakeside,
Mountainside, hillside,
Woodland or grassy plain.
One I consoled –
Black-haired, sad
In her forest clearing –
Another I followed
From a wellspring up in the scree
To a pool's golden rushes.

Did I leave them, forsake them?
I travelled,
Remember no parting.
Ways, I recall, transitions,
The shadows, the colours turning,
Herbs acrid or heady,
Sweet wives the world over,
Sweet virgins walking where they belong –

Unchanged, unchanging regions,
And they unchanged.

But by the knee a stranger
Clawed me, held on;
I fought: my grappling hand
Slid deep into rotten flesh,
A hole behind his ear.
I knocked him down and ran,
Clegs covering me,

A grey crust;
Ran to the church, thinking
They could not enter there,
But still they clung, stinging,
And up I climbed, climbed
To the belfry, pursued
By a man half-decayed.

Sweet wives, sweet virgins
Walk still unchanged,
Do not write, do not miss me,
Never forget.
It was the sunshine, the shadows,
It was the herbs and the haze.

The Blight

Somewhere behind us, from the long room,
Sear-frost, look! cried a child's voice
As fingertips touching we stood
At the window and looked,
Felt the sap run again
From the root up,
New boughs burgeon under the new sun.

Sere-frost, in April?
There it was, icy rain,
And the leaves turned black, curled,
Bud, blossom, shrivelled, fell,
Not one year's growth but the whole tree withered.

Your hand froze in mine,
Froze mine, yet tightened, the nails
Dug in through flesh drained numb,
Dug down to the bones and a deep nerve.

Let go, if you can.

Too slowly toward the root
Our death creeps.

Theogony

One feather, scarlet, on snow:
High rose the bird
That feeds by winter moonlight,
Warbles on farthest mountain tops,
By no man snared, by no man plucked or eaten.

One golden hair
Found on the pillow:
The woman gone, Diana of all that was hers
Grazes with absence the tiled floor
And hallows it, touched by her feet once.

The House Martins

Pines I remember, the air crisp.
Here, in a haze, elms I see,
Do not see, and hills hiding the river.

But the roof is generous,
Can preserve nests. And again the martins mutter
Their small-talk, daily domestic twitter
After those miles, deadly to some,
Over glaciers, over high waves.

Arrived, arrived in whatever wind,
To ride all winds and, housed on the windy side,
Warm with their own blood the cold mud walls.

Cat

Unfussy lodger, she knows what she wants and gets it:
Food, cushions, fires, the run of the garden.
I, her night porter in the small hours
Don't bother to grumble, grimly let her in.
To that coldness she purrs assent,
Eats her fill and outwits me,
Plays hide and seek in the dark house.

Only at times, by chance meeting the gaze
Of her amber eyes that can rest on me
As on a beech-bole, on bracken or meadow grass
I'm moved to celebrate the years between us,
The farness and the nearness:
My fingers graze her head.
To that fondness she purrs assent.

Loach

Loam, slimy loam, embodied, shaped,
Articulate in him. The strength, the softness.
His delicate eye draws light to riverbeds,
Through water draws our weather.

In gravel, mud, he lurks,
Gravel-coloured for safety,
Streamlined only to shoot
Back into mud or merge
In gravel, motionless, lurking.

Low he forages, late,
His radar whiskers alive
To a burrowing worm's commotion,
Tomorrow's thunder;
Advances bounding, prods
And worries a quiet pasture,
Munches athwart, in a cloud.

More than loam, at times he must rise,
His need, his weakness, richly to breathe;
Will rest on weeds, inconspicuous,
But, worse, gulp air, blow bubbles aft,
Expose a belly naked and pale, transparent.
Stickleback, minnow
Gape at his wriggling, uncertain
Whether to nibble or flee.

Perch can swallow him whole.

For A Family Album

Four heads in one lamp's light
And each head bowed into peculiar darkness,
Reading, drawing, alone.
A camera would have caught them, held them there
Half-lit in the room's warm half-light,
Left them, refused to tell
How long till that lamp was broken,
Your hair pinned up or cut or tinted or waved.

I cannot even describe them, caught no more
Than a flash of light that ripped open
The walls of our half-lit room;
Or the negative – a black wedge
Rammed into light so white that it hurt to look.

Leave this page blank.
You'd neither like nor believe
The picture no lens could have taken:

Tied to my rooted bones
In your chairs you were flying, flying.

Friends

1

Here he sits, on the red couch
As twenty years ago on the green or blue
In a different house.
And if I shouted for joy,
Look, we are here, alive,
Wryly, faintly he'd smile:
Not to have died young
Before the dream passed through
Leaving you busy,
You with children about you,
Leaving me
Wherever I may be sitting,
Walking, standing or lying,
Eating, smoking, answering yes or no
Out of the fog, into fog,
Unable to try to remember
What it was like to care
Whether and what I remembered,
Whether and what I tried.
Not to have died young
Means that the couch is red.

2

And I think of another
Who died, with children about him,
Busy always, with words
Neither song nor speech –
Such words
As the dead might use,
Had they breath to waste –

Breathed for the dead.
Between his river, his heron
And the nearest cottage, burnt out,
The hiatus, deathly distance
Bridged by his breathing.

A harpsichord
I remember, never heard him play,
A tiled stove, he stoked it;
Old books, new pictures,
A good face, blurring.
A bundle of letters
I keep, the writing clear
While his hand rots;
And I hear his voice
Clearly, more clearly than
Ever I heard it there
In his room, looking
At the stove, the pictures,
His harpsichord.

3

Our loyalty, old friend, is to the dark
As yet again we walk the same few streets
Past the same grimy hedges,
New cars, new dogs and glossier paint on doors –
Hardly to notice them, or how this wall has crumbled,
But talk as ever of taxes and conscription,
Small victories, small defeats.
And though for twenty-five years you have been saying,
What will become of us,
Too well you know it, meaning not us at all
But his regalia, or else the many things,

Real things, realia of the working day
We care about, only because we know
How poor the realm is, how mad our king.

He dreams, and abdicates,
Leaving no heir, the currency in doubt,
Crying: The King is dead. Long live dead kings –
Lords, by divine right, over dodo and mammoth,
Rulers of nettles, commanders of lava,
Defenders of icebergs adrift in forgotten gales.

Poor capital. Poor streets that still we walk.
Mad king who laughs at those who serve him
And, re-instated, longs for a larger kingdom.
We're nothing in his dream. His dream is ours.

Oxford

Years on the Gothic rack:
Bells crashing down on green water,
Lashing the tree trunks for growing
The meadows for lying flat.

And the flushed girls laughing
At calf love.
Planting banderillas
That itched and dropped, but to burn –
All moved on, moved on

Not where the arches would fling them,
Not to a cloistered garden
Nor yet to the riverside,
The willows, the weeping willows,

To pins and needles in armchairs,
Shrilling of telephone, doorbell,
A well-mannered print or two
Of towers, Gothic, black
Against trim foliage, blue sky.

Teesdale

Walked up to the scar.
Walked down to the beck.
Walked on wet hay, on heather,
On limestone, on spongy grass,
Learning the shapes of tiniest lichen and rock plant,
Marsh crowfoot and meadow campanula,
The various yellows and reds of the monkey flower,
Habitat of juniper, of mountain ash,
Haunts of curlew and grouse,
The wide distribution of starlings.

Bathed in clear shallows, in pools,
In deeper, peat-coloured water.
Saw dawn and dusk, noonlight, moonlight, starlight –
Caught a snatch or two of the small-talk of place.

When the wind began to sing,
Articulate, with human voices from nowhere,
There was an end to small-talk,
Not one peewit to be heard.

When the mist came down
There was no pasture, no copse,
Only the smell of hay getting lost in moorland,
The green and the crimson moss drowning.

Wind and mist –
They took all the rest away.

Oxwich

Wide windscape: the sand moulded
As waves are, into mounds,
But higher, scalloped, rounded
To hold the heat in craters
Walled against winds.
So too birch and ash bend,
Succumb to lichen, salt,
Early stunting, decay;
Brambles crawl, lying low
To save their sparse blue berries,
Intruders here, though prolific
Further back where the tall trees huddle
And the wind's way ends
Up against rock and the rainy hillside.

Long seascape, interlocked
With various land.
Fresh water comes down to brine
From loam through marshland to gravel
And with the lushest warbling
Of blackbird, thrush in warm leaves
Mingles a curlew's fluting
And, windblown, an oystercatcher's;
On shallow banks the footprints,
The detritus of herons, of gulls.

Discount the castle above,
Hidden, and foreign here
As campers who drink a morning
Too bitter-sweet for comfort
Though wind and rain hold back,
A jungle of weeds exhales

Earthy richness beyond the dunes.
Guests at a dangerous marriage
Daily solemnized, broken,
They walk abeyance, close
To whirlpools, to sheer cliffs,
And will not return when the fox
Leanly lopes over ice.

Homo Sum: Humani Nihil Etc.

Too true. Don't say it. Don't.
Trujillo. Hero and owner of a nation,
Honoured and served by men, himself a man,
Upheld, abetted by the lords of commerce,
Dealers in sugar, dealers in carrion –
All men. What else? And the carrion also human.

To be grass, to be cud for cows. Not to know
The taste of meat or the taste of sugar,
To rise again from mud and be green,
Eat mud, eat carrion, but not with a human mouth.

Observer

The newspaper in my hands
Reports a four-sided battle
In the streets of a town
I shall never see.
What I see, what I read
Will depend on this war,
The sum and ratio of men
Maimed or killed on each side.

The newspaper in my hands
Omits to count the losses
On a fifth side – the people.
Yet the winners, if any, will count
The people, if any, left over
Because with no people to rule
The winners would not be the winners,
The war itself would not count.

The newspaper in my hands
Will serve to light a fire,
Yesterday's casualties burn
On my grate tomorrow
Or perhaps with dead leaves in the garden;
Tomorrow's newspaper bring me
Headlines that cancel out
Yesterday's interim score.

The newspaper in my hands
Begins to smoulder, to stink
As I read the day's gossip
About business and fashion,
Parties and mergers and

This gossip-monger's views
On a news handout on
A book on a fashion-pimp.

The newspaper in my hands
Begins to rot my hands.
I drop the newspaper, stare:
From my right forefinger
Something obtrudes. I pinch it
And pull out a worm, then another.
I look at my left hand:
Hollowed out, a black stump.
Amid all those woodlice
Scurrying there I spot
A big slug. With a matchstick held
Between worm-eaten fingers
I spear the slug, remove it.

And nothing hurts. Nothing.

Squares

A misnomer really. With a few exceptions –
The very dumpy and squat – we're rectangular.
Why? Because of our frames, of course:
Invisible frames that expand as we grow.
At times they crack. Then we grow bigger than you.
And even within the frames there's room for big bodies.

The drawbacks? They're obvious. When two of us meet
We rub edges. Round holes give us trouble –
At first, till the frames have ceased to collide.
Most of us, most of the time, are aware of our corners.
That restricts our freedom. We're obsessed with portraits:
Ancestors, heroes, idols, or plain stuffed shirts.

Rectangles rule our lives: when we write poems
They come out as rectangles (not like yours
That zigzag or snake or frogleap all over the place.)
When we dabble in action painting
The frame, foreknown, inhibits our movements.
Coffins too are designed for our frames.

As for you, the smaller of us (the majority)
Hate or envy your guts and your frameless ease;
Frightened, at heart; worried about ourselves;
There's a glut of portraits. The junk yards are full of them,
As the graveyards of coffins, the school anthologies
Of neat rectangular stanzas. What will become of ours?

What will become of you, I wonder. You also proliferate,
Sprawling, slouching, organically squelching and gushing.
Already you look to the East: for flexible frames
That may stiffen with use, if not shrink.
Watch out when corners form. Or all those little old rectangles
Will be gaping and whispering: Did you see that? A square!

New Goddess

I

Mirrors line her shrines,
Full-length, for thighs, knees
To her are dedicated.

Men? They have not been abolished.
Mirrors too their eyes
Can serve the cult

When goddess, priestess in one
She treads profane ground,
Office, pavement, shop floor,

2

Once their domain
Who now are a curious adjunct,
Useful if tame,

As poor cows to farmers once.
Oh, their god's daily tribute
Of grumbles about the cost

Of labourers, winter fodder
And vets! All those male contraptions,
Usable still

Now that farms run themselves
And what with A.I.
One bull goes a long way,

3

Though bulls will slaver, lowing,
Farmers wheedle: love.
How the goddess laughs

Back within her walls
Of pure glass,
Water whose coolness drowned

The boy Narcissus.
Love? The goddess alone
Is a surface-bather,

Surf-riding, wrapped
In her skin of latest cut,
Can dive skin-deep,

4

Keep dry and consort
With mollusc, weed, fish,
Immortal until

Time, their god's invention,
Doled out by farmers once,
Oh, as love too,

Makes heavy with emptiness
Her womb, her breasts,
And the shallows, rippled,

Drag her down, down.

Orpheus Street, S.E. 5

1

Will they move, will they dance,
These houses put up by the money-makers
For the meek, their no-men, to breed in,
Breed money dispersed now, decayed?
And the pawn shop, government surplus,
The cut price petrol station,
Dirty brick, waste paper,
Will his music gather them up?

2

Orpheus transfigures, Orpheus transmutes all things.
His music melts walls. His music wrings
A smile from the lips of killer and nearly killed.
He wills pavements to crack. He whistles at trains,
They whimper, gasp and give up. Wherever 'it' sings
It is Orpheus – with it, well paid for his pains.
Grow, says Orpheus, and dog collars burst,
Tall factories shiver, the whole town swings.

3

Oh, but the traffic diversions.
The road marked World's End, the West,
Runs north and east and south,
And the policeman on duty sneers:
Never mind the direction. You'll get there.
Be courteous. Be patient. If you park,
Your car will be towed away.
If you walk, louts will kick in your ribs.

4

Orpheus is peaceable. Orpheus is faithful
To the woman who was his wife,
Till she suffered a blackout, going
Down, down, where he couldn't reach her,
Where no one belongs to himself,
Far less to another. He lost her;
But loves her still, and loves everyone,
Richly paid for loving.

5

They shriek, they sob for Orpheus,
For a shred of his shirt or flesh.
He turns right, then left,
Proceeds, does a U-turn,
Turns left, turns right, turns left,
The shriek in his ears, everywhere.
He swallows a capsule, prepares
A love song, a peace song, a freedom song.

6

The smile on her face, her smile
When he questioned her eyes for the last time
And she walked away from the stranger.
In halflight he sees no warehouse
But chasms, a river, rock.
A last glint on her hair
And the cave's darkness takes her,
Silent. Silent he leaves.

7

Let lamp posts be trees for once,
Bend their trunks, the park benches
Fling out their limbs, let them fly,
Narrowly missing the sparrows.
Street and mind will not meet
Till street and mind go down
And the footfall that faded, faded,
Draws closer again in the dark,

8

Lamplit or moonlit, his deathland:
Chasms, a river, rock.
The cries of children in alleyways,
The cries of birds in the air,
And the talons, innocent, tearing.
A head will float on foul water
And sing for the rubble, for her,
For the stars, for empty space.

At Fifty-Five

Country dances
Bird calls
The breathing of leaves after thunder –
And now fugues.
Modulations 'impolite'
Syncopations 'unnatural'.
No more clapping of hands
When moonshine had opened their tear-ducts
Or fanfares clenched
Heroic nerves –
But a shaking of heads:
Can't help it, our decomposer,
Can't hear his own blundering discords.

As if one needed ears
For anything but chit-chat about the weather,
Exchange of solicitude, malice –
And birdsong, true, the grosser, the bouncing rhythms.
Uncommunicative? Yes. Unable
'Like beginners to learn from nightingales'.
Unwilling, too, for that matter –
To perform, to rehearse, to repeat,
To take in, to give back.

In time out of time, in the concert no longer concerted.
But the music all there, what music –
Where from –
Water that wells from gravel washed clean by water.
All there – inaudible thrushes
Outsinging the nightingales, peasants
Dancing weightless, without their shoes –
Where from, by what virtue? None.

By what grace but still being here, growing older?
The water cleansed by gravel washed clean by water.

Fugue, ever itself –
And ever growing,
Gathering up – itself,
Plunging – into itself,
Rising – out of itself,
Fathoming – only itself
To end, not to end its flowing –
No longer itself –
In a stillness that never was.

CHARLES TOMLINSON

Sea Change

To define the sea –
We change our opinions
With the changing light.

Light struggles with colour:
A quincunx
Of five stones, a white
Opal threatened by emeralds.

The sea is uneasy marble.

The sea is green silk.

The sea is blue mud, churned
By the insistence of wind.

Beneath dawn a sardonyx may be cut from it
In white layers laced with a carnelian orange,
A leek- or apple-green chalcedony
Hewn in the cold light.

Illustration is white wine
Floating in a saucer of ground glass
On a pedestal of cut glass:

A static instance, therefore untrue.

Observation of Facts

Facts have no eyes. One must
Surprise them, as one surprises a tree
By regarding its (shall I say?)
Facets of copiousness.

The tree stands.

The house encloses.

The room flowers.

These are fact stripped of imagination:
Their relation is mutual.

A dryad is a sort of chintz curtain
Between myself and a tree.
The tree stands: or does not stand:
As I draw, or remove the curtain.

The house encloses: or fails to signify
As being bodied over against one,
As something one has to do with.

The room flowers once one has introduced
Mental fibre beneath its elegance,
A rough pot or two, outweighing
The persistence of frippery
In lampshades or wallpaper.

Style speaks what was seen,
Or it conceals the observation
Behind the observer: a voice
Wearing a ruff.

Those facets of copiousness which I proposed
Exist, do so when we have silenced ourselves.

Dialogue

She: It turns on its axis.

He: To say that it was round
Would be to ignore what is within.
The transparent framework of cells,
The constellation of flashes.

She: It reveals the horizon.

He: It surrounds it,
Transmits and refines it
Through a frozen element:
A taut line crossing a pure white.

She: It contains distance.

He: It distances what is near,
Transforms the conversation piece
Into a still life,
Isolates, like the end of a corridor.

She: It is the world of contour:

He: The black outline separating brilliances
That would otherwise fuse,
A single flame.

She: If it held personages –

He: They would be minute,
Their explicit movements
The mosaic which dances.

Both: In unison, they would clarify
The interior of the fruit,
The heart of the cut stone.

A Meditation on John Constable

Painting is a science, and should be pursued as an inquiry into the laws of nature. Why, then, may not landscape painting be considered as a branch of natural philosophy, of which pictures are but experiments. JOHN CONSTABLE, *The History of Landscape Painting.*

He replied to his own question, and with the unmannered
  Exactness of art; enriched his premises
By confirming his practice: the labour of observation
  In face of meteorological fact. Clouds
Followed by others, temper the sun in passing
  Over and off it. Massed darks
Blotting it back, scattered and mellowed shafts
  Break damply out of them, until the source
Unmasks, floods its retreating bank
  With raw fire. One perceives (though scarcely)
The remnant clouds trailing across it
  In rags, and thinned to a gauze.
But the next will dam it. They loom past
  And narrow its blaze. It shrinks to a crescent
Crushed out, a still lengthening ooze
  As the mass thickens, though cannot exclude
Its silvered-yellow. The eclipse is sudden,
  Seen first on the darkening grass, then complete
In a covered sky.
                    Facts. And what are they?
He admired accidents, because governed by laws,
  Representing them (since the illusion was not his end)
As governed by feeling. The end is our approval
  Freely accorded, the illusion persuading us
That it exists as a human image. Caught
  By a wavering sun, or under a wind
Which moistening among the outlines of banked foliage
  Prepares to dissolve them, it must grow constant;

Though there, ruffling and parted, the disturbed
  Trees let through the distance, like white fog
Into their broken ranks. It must persuade
  And with a constancy, not to be swept back
To reveal what it half-conceals. Art is itself
  Once we accept it. The day veers. He would have judged
Exactly in such a light, that strides down
  Over the quick stains of cloud-shadows
Expunged now, by its conflagration of colour.
  A descriptive painter? If delight
Describes, which wrings from the brush
  The errors of a mind, so tempered,
It can forgo all pathos; for what he saw
  Discovered what he was, and the hand – unswayed
By the dictation of a single sense –
  Bodied the accurate and total knowledge
In a calligraphy of present pleasure. Art
  Is complete when it is human. It is human
Once the looped pigments, the pin-heads of light
  Securing space under their deft restrictions
Convince, as the index of a possible passion,
  As the adequate gauge, both of the passion
And its object. The artist lies
  For the improvement of truth. Believe him.

The Crane

That insect, without antennae, over its
Cotton-spool lip, letting
An almost invisible tenuity
Of steel cable, drop
Some seventy feet, with the
Grappling hook hidden also
Behind a dense foreground
Among which it is fumbling, and
Over which, mantis-like
It is begging or threatening, gracile
From a clear sky – that paternal
Constructive insect, without antennae,
Would seem to assure us that
'The future is safe, because
It is in my hands.' And we do not
Doubt this veracity, we can only
Fear it – as many of us
As pause here to remark
Such silent solicitude
For lifting intangible weights
Into real walls.

Oxen: Ploughing at Fiesole

The heads, impenetrable
And the slow bulk
Soundless and stooping,
A white darkness – burdened
Only by sun, and not
By the matchwood yoke –
They groove in ease
The meadow through which they pace
Tractable. It is as if
Fresh from the escape,
They consent to submission,
The debris of captivity
Still clinging there
Unnoticed behind those backs:
'But we submit' – the tenor
Unambiguous in that stride
Of even confidence –
'Giving and not conceding
Your premises. Work
Is necessary, therefore – '
(With an unsevered motion
Holding the pauses
Between stride and stride)
'We will be useful
But we will not be swift: now
Follow us for your improvement
And at our pace.' This calm
Bred from this strength, and the reality
Broaching no such discussion,
The man will follow, each
As the other's servant
Content to remain content.

Glass Grain

The glare goes down. The metal of a molten pane
Cast on the wall with red light burning through,
Holds in its firm, disordered square, the shifting strands
The glass conceals, till (splitting sun) it dances,
Lanterns in lanes of light its own streaked image.
Like combed-down hair. Like weathered wood, where
Line, running with, crowds on line and swaying
Rounding each knot, yet still keeps keen
The perfect parallel. Like . . . in likes, what do we look for?
Distinctions? That, but not that in sum. Think of the
fugue's theme:

After inversions and divisions, doors
That no keys can open, cornered conceits
Apprehensions, all ways of knowledge past,
Eden comes round again, the motive dips
Back to its shapely self, its naked nature
Clothed by comparison alone – related. We ask
No less, watching suggestions that a beam selects
From wood, from water, from a muslin-weave,
Swerving across our window, on our wall
(Transparency teased out) the grain of glass.

The Ruin

Dissolving, the coals shift. Rain swaddles us
And the fire, driving its shadows through the room
Recalls us to our intention as the flames
That, by turns, sink guttering or mount
To pour red light through every crater,
Threaten the galleries of crumbling ash.

The ruins sag, then sift downwards,
Their fall so soundless that, for the first time,
We distinguish the unbroken, muffled sibilance
Rain has accompanied us with. Our talk
Recovers its theme – the ruin we should have visited
Abandoned, now, in its own emptiness.

For the morning promised what, through the darkening air,
Afternoon retracted, nor will the evening
Welcome us under its turmoil of wet leaves
Where we have lost the keenness of such acridity
As a burnt ruin exhales long afterwards
Into the coolness when rain has ceased.

It stands on the hill slope. Between green and green
There is the boundary wall that circles
And now hides it. Within, one can see nothing
Save the third, chequered indefinite green
Of treetops – until, skirting these limits
One discovers, open upon the emptied confine, the gate.

For a week, the swift traffic of demolition
That mottled with oil their stagnant rain,
Advanced through the deepening ruts,
Converged on the house, disjointed, reassembled

And carted, flung (what had sprawled unhinged)
  The door into the wreckage and burnt both.

The door which, though elegant, leaned from the true
  A little to one side, was shamed
By the nearby, slender but rigid elm –
  An unchanging comedy, varied
Only as the seasons thought fit and as the days
  Under their shifting lights reviewed it.

The house was not ancient, but old: deserted,
  The slewed door had focused its rotting style
And, as proportion tugged from decrepitude
  A faint self-respect, it was the door
With the firmness of an aged but practised arbiter
  Bestowed it back over the entire ruin.

Impartial with imperfections, it could accuse
  By this scant presence its clustering neighbours
Gross with the poverty of utility. Thus challenging, it stayed,
  A problem for the authorities, a retreat for urchins
Until the urchins burnt half and the authorities
  Publicly accomplished what their ally had attempted by stealth.
There remains now the levelled parapet of earth,
  The bleak diagram of a foundation, a hearth
Focusing nothing and, cast into it, the filigree ghost
  Of an iron fanlight. Could we assemble
Beside its other fragments, that last grace
  Under this meaner roof, they would accuse us still –

And accusing, speak from beyond their dereliction
Out of their life; as when a vase
Cracked into shards, would seem
Baldly to confess, 'Men were here',
The arabesque reproves it, tracing in faint lines:
'Ceremonies and order were here also.'

Nor could we answer: our houses
Are no longer ourselves; they dare not
Enter our hopes as the guests of meditation
To reanimate, warmed by this contact,
The laric world where the bowl glistens with presence
Gracing the table on which it unfolds itself.

Thus fire, renewed at our hearth, consumes.
Yet it cannot create from the squalor of moderation
A more than fortuitous glory, multiplying its image
Over the projections of lacquered wood. Charged with their past,
Those relics smoulder before they are compounded
And turned by the spade under a final neatness.

The window lightens. The shell parts
Beyond between cloud and sky line.
Thunder-light, flushing the walls, yellows them
Into a more ardent substance than their own
And can do no more. The effect is nature's
Who ignores it, and in whose impoverishment we domicile.

Winter Encounters

House and hollow; village and valley-side:
  The ceaseless pairings, the interchange
In which the properties are constant
  Resumes its winter starkness. The hedges' barbs
Are bared. Lengthened shadows
  Intersecting, the fields seem parcelled smaller
As if by hedgerow within hedgerow. Meshed
  Into neighbourhood by such shifting ties,
The house reposes, squarely upon its acre
  Yet with softened angles, the responsive stone
Changeful beneath the changing light:
  There is a riding-forth, a voyage impending
In this ruffled air, where all moves
  Towards encounter. Inanimate or human,
The distinction fails in these brisk exchanges –
  Say, merely, that the roof greets the cloud,
Or by the wall, sheltering its knot of talkers,
  Encounter enacts itself in the conversation
On customary subjects, where the mind
  May lean at ease, weighing the prospect
Of another's presence. Rain
  And the probability of rain, tares
And their progress through a field of wheat –
  These, though of moment in themselves,
Serve rather to articulate the sense
  That having met, one meets with more
Than the words can witness. One feels behind
  Into the intensity that bodies through them
Calmness within the wind, the warmth in cold.

CHARLES TOMLINSON

Sea Poem

A whiter bone:
the sea-voice
in a multiple monody
crowding towards that end.
It is as if
the transparencies of sound
composing such whiteness
disposed many layers
with a sole movement
of the various surface,
the depths, bottle-glass green
the bed, swaying
like a fault in the atmosphere, each
shift
with its separate whisper, each whisper
a breath of that singleness
that 'moves together
if it moves at all',
and its movement is ceaseless,
and to one end –
the grinding
a whiter bone.

The Tree

I had seen a tree before,
the amputated trunk
merely a table-top
set on a single claw
of roots. But that
was not like this:
this lay awry
even before they cut it;
this – propped up
on the elbows of its boughs
– spanned half a hill
and bridged the green
dank slot
a narrow stream
had worn into the flank
beyond. On end
it leaned against
the rising slope.
Leafless? It was never
leafless. Leaves
climbed with it, roots
socketed and spread into
the layered marl.
And leaves were on it now
that pierced the air
with crumpled wedges –
you could sense the injury
in that half-completed gesture
and before you knew
the cause of it.
This might have seemed
an occasion for regret,

had not the effect
been incontestable.
The saw had entered
sideways the knot of roots,
and the plane it left,
resistant, vertical,
exposed a map
of grains and stains,
a mud-splashed
scored relief
held by a frame,
an inlay lip,
where the rind enclosed it.
The sections of the trunk
greeted each other
from opposing banks
nakedly. A third
irregularly fluted,
now erect,
completed the triangulation,
tugged the group
afresh into a unity
from where it stood
and finally a rain
had cleansed it, freshened,
flushed the colour through.
The reservoir of cóntent,
dammed behind
the mask of form,
the tree's geometry
still put the same
unanswerable question
as the living tree,
though framed it

with a difference, and I
between its Janus faces,
was compelled to echo it,
as though the repetition could
reconsecrate this altar of discarded wood.

Black Nude

A night-bound fire,
Its cloudy, twisting bulk
Of climbing smoke
Lit by the under-flare:
She stretches, strong
And turning there, recalls it.

All sullen force. What
Can such powers rehearse
Shut in themselves? But see
Her rouse and go
Towards the defining window's
Square of sky.

Less sulkily, the silhouette
Looks out and down
On to the town of roofs
In patterned alternation where
Hard dark is buttressed by hard glare.

Her face receives the sun
And softens it. Angled by
Her arm's embrasure,
White architectured distances
Ride sleeping in the clear truce of her eye.

The Crow

The inspecting eye
shows cold
amid the head's
disquieted iridescence.
The whole bird sits
rocking at a vantage
clumsily. The glance
alone is steady
and a will behind it
rights the stance,
corrects all disposition
to ungainly action.
Acting, it will be
as faultless as its eye
in a concerted drop
on carrion; or watch
it fly – the insolence
transfers to wing-tip
and the action wears
an ease that's merciless,
all black assumption,
mounting litheness.
The blown bird,
inaccessible its intimations
of the wind, 'Stay
where you are' is
what it says and we
poor swimmers
in that element
stay, to bear
with clumsy eye
affronted witness at its ways in air.

The Hand at Callow Hill Farm

Silence. The man defined
The quality, ate at his separate table
Silent, not because silence was enjoined
But was his nature. It shut him round
Even at outdoor tasks, his speech
Following upon a pause, as though
A hesitance to comply had checked it –
Yet comply he did, and willingly:
Pause and silence: both
Were essential graces, a reticence
Of the blood, whose calm concealed
The tutelary of that upland field.

John Maydew or *the Allotment*

Ranges
 of clinker heaps
  go orange now:
through cooler air
 an acrid drift
  seeps upwards
from the valley mills;
 the spoiled and staled
  distances invade
these closer comities
 of vegetable shade,
  glass-houses, rows
and trellises of red-
 ly flowering beans.
  This
is a paradise
 where you may smell
  the cinders
of quotidian hell beneath you;
 here grow
  their green reprieves
for those
 who labour, linger in
  their watch-chained waistcoats
rolled-back sleeves –
 the ineradicable
  peasant in the dispossessed
and half-tamed Englishman.
 By day, he makes
  a burrow of necessity
from which
 at evening, he emerges

here.
A thoughtful yet unthinking man,
John Maydew,
memory stagnates
in you and breeds
a bitterness; it grew
and rooted in your silence
from the day
you came
unwitting out of war
in all the pride
of ribbons and a scar
to forty years
of mean amends . . .
He squats
within his shadow
and a toad
that takes
into a slack and twitching jaw
the worms he proffers it,
looks up at him
through eyes that are
as dimly faithless
as the going years.
For, once returned
he found that he
must choose between
an England, profitlessly green
and this –
a seamed and lunar grey
where slag in lavafolds
unrolls beneath him.
The valley gazes up
through kindling eyes

as, unregarded at his back,
    its hollows deepen
        with the black, extending shadows
and the sounds of day
    explore its coming cavities,
        the night's
refreshed recesses.
    Tomorrow
        he must feed its will,
his interrupted pastoral
    take heart into
        those close
and gritty certainties that lie
    a glowing ruse
        all washed in hesitations now.
He eyes the toad
    beating
        in the assuagement
of his truce.

Arizona Desert

Eye
drinks the dry orange ground,
the cowskull
bound to it by shade:
sun-warped, the layers
of flaked and broken bone
unclench into petals,
into eyelids of limestone:

Blind glitter
that sees
spaces and steppes expand
of the purgatories possible
to us and
impossible.

Upended trees
in the Hopi's desert orchard
betoken
unceasing unspoken war,
return
the levelling light,
imageless arbiter.

A dead snake
pulsates again
as, hidden, the beetles' hunger
mines through the tunnel of its drying skin.

Here, to be,
is to sound
patience deviously
and follow
like the irregular corn
the water underground.

Villages
from mud and stone
parch back
to the dust they humanize
and mean
marriage, a loving lease
on sand, sun, rock and
Hopi
means peace.

CHARLES TOMLINSON

A Death in the Desert

IN MEMORY OF HOMER VANCE

There are no crosses
on the Hopi graves. They lie
shallowly
under a scattering
of small boulders. The sky
over the desert
with its sand-grain stars
and the immense equality
between
desert and desert sky,
seem
a scope and ritual
enough to stem
death and to be its equal.

'Homer
is the name,' said
the old Hopi doll-maker.
I met him in summer. He was dead
when I came back that autumn.

He had sat
like an Olympian
in his cool room
on the rock-roof of the world,
beyond the snatch
of circumstance
and was to die
beating a burro out of his corn-patch.

'That,'
said his neighbour
'was a week ago'. And the week
that lay
uncrossably between us
stretched into sand,
into the spread
of the endless
waterless sea-bed beneath
whose space outpacing sight
receded as speechless and as wide as death.

CHARLES TOMLINSON

The Well

IN A MEXICAN CONVENT

Leaning on
the parapet stone
Listening down
the long, dark
sheath through which the standing
shaft of water
sends its echoings up
Catching, as it stirs
the steady seethings
that mount and mingle
with surrounding sounds
from the neighbouring
barrack-yard: soldiery
– heirs, no doubt
of the gunnery that gashed
these walls of tattered
frescoes, the bullet-
holes now socketed
deeper by sunlight
and the bright gaps
giving on to the square
and there revealing
strollers in khaki
with their girls Aware
of a well-like
cool throughout
the entire, clear
sunlit ruin,
of the brilliant cupids
above the cistern
that hold up

a baldachin of stone
which is not there
Hearing the tide
of insurrection
 subside through time
under the still-
painted slogans
 Hemos servido
lealmente
la revolución

CHARLES TOMLINSON

Weeper in Jalisco

A circle of saints, all
hacked, mauled, bound,
bleed in a wooden frieze
under the gloom of the central
dome of gold. They
are in paradise now
and we are not –
baroque feet gone
funnelling up, a blood-
bought, early resurrection
leaving us this
tableau of wounds, the crack
in the universe sealed
behind their flying backs.
We are here, and a woman
sprawls and wails to them
there, the gold screen
glistening, hemming her
under, till her keening
fills the stone ear
of the whole, hollow sanctum
and she is the voice
those wounds cry through
unappeasably bleeding where
her prone back shoulders
the price and weight
of forfeited paradise.

In Connecticut

White, these villages. White
their churches without altars. The first snow
falls through a grey-white sky
and birch-twig whiteness turns
whiter against the grey. White
the rows of pillars (each
of them is a single tree), the walls
sculptureless. 'This church was gathered
in 1741. In 1742
by act of the General Assembly of Connecticut
this territory was incorporated
and was named Judea.'
The sun passes, the elms
enter as lace shadows, then
go out again. White . . .
'Our minister is fine. He's a minister
in church, and a man outside.' – delivered
with the same shadowless conviction
as her invitation, when
lowering, leaning
out of the window she was cleaning
she had said: 'Our doors
are always open.'

CHARLES TOMLINSON

A Garland for Thomas Eakins

I

He lived
from his second year
at seventeen twentynine
Mount Vernon Street
Philadelphia
Pennsylvania where
he painted his
father and his sisters
and he died
in Pennsylvania in
Philadelphia at
seventeen twentynine
Mount Vernon Street.

2

Anatomy, perspective
and reflection: a boat
in three inclinations:
to the wind, to the waves
and to the picture-frame.
Those are the problems. What
does a body propose
that a boat does not?

3

Posing the model
for 'The Concert Singer' he
stood her
relative to a grid
placed vertically

behind her. There was a spot
before her
on the wall that
she must look at.
To her dress
by the intersections
of the grid he tied
coloured ribbons, thus
projecting her
like an architect's elevation
on a plane
that was vertical, the canvas
at a right angle
to the eye and perpendicular
to the floor.
What does the man
who sees
trust to
if not the eye? He trusts
to knowledge
to right appearances.

4

– And what do you think of
that, Mr. Eakins? (A Whistler)
– I think that that
is a very cowardly way to paint.

5

A fat woman
by Rubens
is not a fat
woman but a fiction.

6

The Eakins portrait
(said Whitman)
sets me down
in correct style
without feathers.
And when they
said to him:
Has Mr. Eakins no
social gifts? he said
to them: What are
'social gifts'? –
The parlour puts
quite its own
measure upon social gifts.

7

The figures of perception
as against
the figures of elocution.
What they wanted
was to be Medici
in Philadelphia
and they survive
as Philadelphians.

8

The accord with that
which asked
only to be recorded:
'How beautiful,' he said,
'an old lady's skin is:
all those wrinkles!'

9

Only
to be recorded!
and his stare
in the self-portrait
calculates the abyss
in the proposition. He dies
unsatisfied, born
to the stubborn
anguish of
those eyes.

CHARLES TOMLINSON

Idyll

WASHINGTON SQUARE, SAN FRANCISCO

A door:
    PER L'UNIVERSO
        is what it says
above it.
    You must approach
        more nearly
(the statue
    of Benjamin Franklin watching you)
        before you see
La Gloria di Colui
    che tutto muove
        PER L'UNIVERSO
– leaning
    along the lintel –
        penetra e risplende
across this church
    for Italian Catholics:
        Dante
unscrolling in rhapsody.
    Cool
        the January sun,
that with an intensity
    the presence of the sea
        makes more exact,
chisels the verse with shade
    and lays
        on the grass
a deep and even
    Californian green,
        while a brilliance

throughout the square
  flatters the meanness of its architecture.
    Beyond
there is the flood
  which skirts this pond
    and tugs the ear
towards it: cars
  thick on the gradients of the city
    shift sun and sound –
a constant ground-bass
  to these provincialisms of the piazza
    tasting still
of Lerici and Genova.
  Here
    as there
the old men sit
  in a mingled odour
    of cheroot and garlic
spitting;
  they share serenity
    with the cross-legged
Chinese adolescent
  seated between them
    reading, and whose look
wears the tranquillity of consciousness
  forgotten in its object –
    his book
bears for a title
  SUCCESS
    in spelling.
How
  does one spell out this
    che penetra e risplende
from square

into the hill-side alley-ways
around it, where
between tall houses
children of the Mediterranean
and Chinese element
mingle
their American voices? . . .
The dictionary
defines idyllium
as meaning
'a piece, descriptive
chiefly of rustic life';
we
are in town: here
let it signify
this poised quiescence, pause
and possibility in which
the music of the generations
binds into its skein
the flowing instant,
while the winter sun
pursues the shadow
before a church
whose decoration
is a quotation from *Paradiso.*

The Door

Too little
has been said
of the door, its one
face turned to the night's
downpour and its other
to the shift and glisten of firelight.

Air, clasped
by this cover
into the room's book,
is filled by the turning
pages of dark and fire
as the wind shoulders the panels, or unsteadies that burning.

Not only
the storm's
breakwater, but the sudden
frontier to our concurrences, appearances,
and as full of the offer of space
as the view through a cromlech is.

For doors
are both frame and monument
to our spent time,
and too little
has been said
of our coming through and leaving by them.

The Weathercocks

Bitten and burned into mirrors of thin gold,
the weathercocks, blind from the weather,
have their days of seeing as they
grind round on their swivels.

A consciousness of pure metal
begins to melt when (say)
that light 'which never was'
begins to be

And catches the snow's accents
in each dip and lap, and the wide
stains on the thawed ploughland are like continents
across a rumpled map.

Their gold eyes hurt
at the corduroy lines come clear whose grain
feels its way over the shapes of the rises
joining one brown accord of stain and stain.

And the patterning stretches, flown
out on a wing of afternoon cloud that the sun
is changing to sea-wet sandflats,
hummocked in tiny dunes like the snow half-gone –

As if the sole wish of the light
were to harrow with mind matter, to shock
wide the glance of the tree-knots and the stone-eyes
the sun is bathing, to waken the weathercocks.

On the Principle of Blowclocks: three way poem

The static forces
not a ball of silver
of a solid body
but a ball of air
and its material strength
whose globed sheernesses
derive from
shine with a twofold glitter:
not the quantity of mass:
once with the dew and once
an engineer would instance
with the constituent bright threads
rails or T beams, say
of all its spokes
four planes constructed to
in a tense surface
contain the same volume as
in a solid cloud of stars
four tons of mass

Words for the Madrigalist

Look with the ears, said Orazio Vecchi,
  Trusting to music, willing to be led
Voluntarily blind through its complete
  Landscape of the emotion, feeling beneath the feet
Of the mind's heart, the land fall, the height
  Re-form: Look with the ears – they are all
Looking with the eyes, missing the way:
  So, waiting for sleep, I look
With the ears at the confused clear sounds
  As each replenished tributary unwinds
Its audible direction, and dividing
  The branchwork of chime and counterchime
Runs the river's thick and drumming stem:
  Loud with their madrigal of limestone beds
Where nothing sleeps, they all
  Give back – not the tune the listener calls
But the measure of what he is
  In the hard, sweet music of his lack,
The unpremeditated consonances: and the words
  Return it to you over the ground-
Bass of their syllables, Orazio Vecchi:
  Hear with the eyes as you catch the current of their sounds.

Clouds

How should the dreamer, on those slow
  Solidities, fix his wandering adagio,
Seizing, bone-frail, blown
  Through the diaphanous air of their patrols,
Shadows of fanfares, grails of melting snow?
  How can he hope to hold that white
Opacity as it endures, advances,
  At a dream's length? Its strength
Confounds him with detail, his glance falls
  From ridge to ridge down the soft canyon walls,
And, fleece as it may seem, its tones
  And touch are not the fleece of dream,
But light and body, spaced accumulation
  The mind can take its purchase on:
Cloudshapes are destinies, and they
  Charging the atmosphere of a common day,
Make it the place of confrontation where
  The dreamer wakes to the categorical call
And clear cerulean trumpet of the air.

Swimming Chenango Lake

Winter will bar the swimmer soon.
  He reads the water's autumnal hesitations
A wealth of ways: it is jarred,
  It is astir already despite its steadiness,
Where the first leaves at the first
  Tremor of the morning air have dropped
Anticipating him, launching their imprints
  Outwards in eccentric, overlapping circles.
There is a geometry of water, for this
  Squares off the clouds' redundances
And sets them floating in a nether atmosphere
  All angles and elongations: every tree
Appears a cypress as it stretches there
  And every bush that shows the season,
A shaft of fire. It is a geometry and not
  A fantasia of distorting forms, but each
Liquid variation answerable to the theme
  It makes away from, plays before:
It is a consistency, the grain of the pulsating flow.
  But he has looked long enough, and now
Body must recall the eye to its dependence
  As he scissors the waterscape apart
And sways it to tatters. Its coldness
  Holding him to itself, he grants the grasp,
For to swim is also to take hold
  On water's meaning, to move in its embrace
And to be, between grasp and grasping free.
  He reaches in-and-through to that space
The body is heir to, making a where
  In water, a possession to be relinquished
Willingly at each stroke. The image he has torn
  Flows-to behind him, healing itself,

Lifting and lengthening, splayed like the feathers
  Down an immense wing whose darkening spread
Shadows his solitariness: alone, he is unnamed
  By this baptism, where only Chenango bears a name
In a lost language he begins to construe –
  A speech of densities and derisions, of half-
Replies to the questions his body must frame
  Frogwise across the all but penetrable element.
Human, he fronts it and, human, he draws back
  From the interior cold, the mercilessness
That yet shows a kind of mercy sustaining him.
  The last sun of the year is drying his skin
Above a surface a mere mosaic of tiny shatterings,
  Where a wind is unscaping all images in the flowing obsidian,
The going-elsewhere of ripples incessantly shaping.

CHARLES TOMLINSON

The Fox Gallery

A long house –
the fox gallery you called
its upper storey, because
you could look down to see
(and did) the way a fox would
cross the field beyond
and you could follow out, window
to window, the fox's way
the whole length of the meadow
parallel with the restraining line
of wall and pane, or as far
as that could follow the sense of all
those windings. Do you remember
the morning I woke you with the cry
Fox fox and the animal
came on – not from side
to side, but straight
at the house and we craned
to see more and more, the most
we could of it and then
watched it sheer off deterred
by habitation, and saw
how utterly the two worlds were
disparate, as that perfect
ideogram for agility
and liquefaction flowed
away from us rhythmical
and flickering and
that flare was final.

Against Extremity

Let there be treaties, bridges,
  Chords under the hands, to be spanned
Sustained: extremity hates a given good
  Or a good gained. That girl who took
Her life almost, then wrote a book
  To exorcise and to exhibit the sin,
Praises a friend there for the end she made
  And each of them becomes a heroine.
The time is in love with endings. The time's
  Spoiled children threaten what they will do,
And those they cannot shake by petulance
  They'll bribe out of their wits by show.
Against extremity, let there be
  Such treaties as only time itself
Can ratify, a bond and test
  Of sequential days, and like the full
Moon slowly given to the night,
  A possession that is not to be possessed.

Prometheus

Summer thunder darkens, and its climbing
  Cumulae, disowning our scale in the zenith,
Electrify this music: the evening is falling apart.
  Castles-in-air; on earth: green, livid fire.
The radio simmers with static to the strains
  Of this mock last-day of nature and of art.

We have lived through apocalypse too long:
  Scriabin's dinosaurs! Trombones for the transformation
That arrived by train at the Finland Station,
  To bury its hatchet after thirty years in the brain
Of Trotsky. Alexander Nikolayevitch, the events
  Were less merciful than your mob of instruments.

Too many drowning voices cram this waveband.
  I set Lenin's face by yours –
Yours, the fanatic ego of eccentricity against
  The systematic son of a schools inspector
Tyutchev on desk – for the strong man reads
  Poets as the antisemite pleads: 'A Jew was my friend.'

Cymballed firesweeps. Prometheus came down
  In more than orchestral flame and Kerensky fled
Before it. The babel of continents gnaws now
  And tears at the silk of those harmonies that seemed
So dangerous once. You dreamed an end
  Where the rose of the world would go out like a close in
      music.

Population drags the partitions down
  And we are a single town of warring suburbs:
I cannot hear such music for its consequence:

Each sense was to have been reborn
Out of a storm of perfumes and light
To a white world, an in-the-beginning.

In the beginning, the strong man reigns:
Trotsky, was it not then you brought yourself
To judgement and to execution, when you forgot
Where terror rules, justice turns arbitrary?
Chromatic Prometheus, myth of fire,
It is history topples you in the zenith.

Blok, too, wrote The Scythians
Who should have known: he who howls
With the whirlwind, with the whirlwind goes down.
In this, was Lenin guiltier than you
When, out of a merciless patience grew
The daily prose such poetry prepares for?

Scriabin, Blok, men of extremes,
History treads out the music of your dreams
Through blood, and cannot close like this
In the perfection of anabasis. It stops. The trees
Continue raining though the rain has ceased
In a cooled world of incessant codas:

Hard edges of the houses press
On the after-music senses, and refuse to burn,
Where an ice-cream van circulates the estate
Playing Greensleeves, and at the city's
Stale new frontier even ugliness
Rules with the cruel mercy of solidities.

MORE ABOUT PENGUINS

Penguinews, which appears every month, contains details of all the new books issued by Penguins as they are published. From time to time it is supplemented by *Penguins in Print* – a complete list of all our available titles. (There are well over three thousand of these.)

A specimen copy of *Penguinews* will be sent to you free on request, and you can become a subscriber for the price of the postage – 4s. for a year's issues (including the complete lists) if you live in the United Kingdom, or 8s. if you live elsewhere. Just write to Dept EP, Penguin Books Ltd, Harmondsworth, Middlesex, enclosing a cheque or postal order, and your name will be added to the mailing list.

Some other Penguin poetry is listed on the following pages.

Note: *Penguinews* and *Penguins in Print* are not available in the U.S.A. or Canada

Some Penguin poetry translated by Michael Hamburger

HANS MAGNUS ENZENSBERGER*

This selection draws on Hans Magnus Enzensberger's three published volumes and also includes a number of other poems. The poet is a German – although uniquely cosmopolitan in outlook and range of sympathies – who was shaped by the Second World War and who expresses an awareness of the ideology responsible for that war and of the breakdown which followed it. His social and moral criticism owes much to Marxism, yet is free from party allegiance. As direct and accessible as graffiti on a wall, his poems are the most striking to emerge from post-war Germany.

GÜNTER GRASS*

Günter Grass, famous as a novelist, is here presented as a poet in a selection from his three published volumes. Grass's belief that an artist, however committed he may be in life, should be only a jester in art, is admirably practised in these poems in which fantasy, ingenuity and humour are substitutes for didacticism, and no word, thing or idea is too sacrosanct to be played with. Even in the recent controversial political poems, which come close to blurring his division between life and art, Grass's tremendous zest and sensuous response are felt.

and

GERMAN WRITING TODAY

Edited by Christopher Middleton

THE PENGUIN MODERN POETS

*THE PENGUIN MODERN POETS 1

Lawrence Durrell, Elizabeth Jennings, and R. S. Thomas

*THE PENGUIN MODERN POETS 2

Kingsley Amis, Dom Moraes, and Peter Porter

*THE PENGUIN MODERN POETS 3

George Barker, Martin Bell, and Charles Causley

*THE PENGUIN MODERN POETS 4

David Holbrook, Christopher Middleton, and David Wevill

†THE PENGUIN MODERN POETS 5

Lawrence Ferlinghetti, Allen Ginsberg, and Gregory Corso

THE PENGUIN MODERN POETS 6

George MacBeth, Edward Lucie-Smith, and Jack Clemo

*THE PENGUIN MODERN POETS 7

Richard Murphy, Jon Silkin, and Nathaniel Tarn

*THE PENGUIN MODERN POETS 8

Edwin Brock, Geoffrey Hill, and Stevie Smith

†THE PENGUIN MODERN POETS 9

Denise Levertov, Kenneth Rexroth, and William Carlos Williams

THE PENGUIN MODERN POETS 10

Adrian Henri, Roger McGough, and Brian Patten

THE PENGUIN MODERN POETS 11

D. M. Black, Peter Redgrove, and D. M. Thomas

*THE PENGUIN MODERN POETS 12

Alan Jackson, Jeff Nuttall, and William Wantling

THE PENGUIN MODERN POETS 13

Charles Bukowski, Philip Lamantia, and Harold Norse

THE PENGUIN MODERN POETS 15

Alan Bold, Edward Brathwaite, Edwin Morgan

THE PENGUIN MODERN POETS 16

Jack Beeching, Harry Guest, Matthew Mead

**Not for sale in the U.S.A.* *†Not for sale in the U.S.A. or Canada*